MW01222997

Great
SHORT
POEMS
from
Around the World

Great
SHORT
POEMS
from
Around the World

Edited by
Bob Blaisdell

DOVER PUBLICATIONS, INC.
Mineola, New York

ACKNOWLEDGMENTS: see page xxv.

The publisher gratefully acknowledges the generous assistance of
Dorothy Belle Pollack in the preparation and
selection of poems for this volume.

Copyright

Bibliographical Note

Great Short Poems from Around the World is a new compilation, first published by
Dover Publications, Inc., in 2013.

Library of Congress Cataloging-in-Publication Data

Great short poems from around the world / edited by Bob Blaisdell.
   p. cm.
  Includes index.
  ISBN-13: 978-0-486-47877-7
  ISBN-10: 0-486-47877-7
  1. Poetry—Collections.   2. Poetry—Translations into English.   I. Blaisdell,
Robert.
  PN6101.G72 2013
  808.81—dc22

2011010017

Manufactured in the United States by Courier Corporation
47877701   2013
www.doverpublications.com

Note

Wouldst thou hear what man can say
In a little? reader, stay.
                 — Ben Jonson

We'll keep this short.

There is no genre of poetry called "short," exactly, though there are many short-forms. Most poetry simply *is* short and takes only a minute or two to slide or slog through. But "short" for this volume means "100 syllables or less." When I found several translations of "My muse, what ails this ardor?" by Sappho, the greatest lyric poet of ancient Greece, only one of them in English translation squeezed under the syllable limit, and that was by the most stupendous sonneteer in English literary history, Sir Philip Sidney. (Speaking of Sidney's great sonnets, at 140 syllables they are way, way too long.) I have avoided clipping sparkling lines and stanzas from the world's great poets because I wanted to present poems that were written short — that said what had to be said, *just like that!*, and then out the door. Perhaps it's no coincidence that there are an awful lot of short poems describing the passions aroused and provoked by the lightning strikes of romantic love: jealousy, misery, disappointment, delight, joy, comfort, bliss:

> Unhappy they whose life is loveless;
>> for without love
>>> it is not easy to do aught or to say aught.

I, for example, am now all too slow,
    but were I to catch sight of Xenophilus
      I would fly swifter than lightning.

Therefore I bid all men not to shun
    but to pursue sweet desire;
      Love is the whetstone of the soul.

   —Alpheius of Mytilene

How to catch such feelings except in a few ecstatic lines? There are not so many philosophical poems as love poems, if only because philosophy usually needs explanation. There are poems of grief and remembrance, and many extremely short poems of quiet perfect observation:

A fallen blossom
    returning to the bough, I thought—
But no, a butterfly.

   —Arakida Moritake

While these poems do come from all around the world, it happens that some cultures have favored genres that extend poetry into forms that couldn't be called short. On the other hand, the Japanese developed and mastered haiku while the classical Romans and Greeks cultivated epigrams. If that sounds like an apology that there seem too few poems from, for example, South America, Africa, and Malaysia, among many other regions of the world, it *is*. Someone else could do an anthology with an equal number of poems in English, using the same syllable limit, and not include a single poem that's in this one and have just as worthy a collection. This means that there are jewels upon jewels of short poems the world over and these are just a few hundred I encountered on my treasure hunt.

Finally I must explain or excuse the alphabetical arrangement of this anthology; my hopes are that the randomness of our alphabet will keep the reader's focus on the "short" form rather than on country of origin, language, or chronology, which would suggest *development* across time, culture, language, and space rather than on how individual poets do their best to make an impressive little something out of a few syllables. (By the way, some of the poets with Arabic names are alphabetized by first name if it is their family name—for example: "*Abu'l-Ala al-Ma'rri.*") I'm pleased with the happy arrangement that sits Ezra Pound at the table next to Alexander Pushkin or Emily Dickinson followed by the Indian Dilsoz. I am aware of having made occasional anachronistic identifications of country of origin for each poet. Sappho, a native of the island of Lesbos, wrote in Greek but wouldn't have thought of herself as living in "Greece." Rainer Maria Rilke, born in Prague, part of the Austro-Hungarian "Bohemia" at the time, wrote in German but lived for various periods all over Europe. The Latin poet Martial was from an area in present-day Spain but lived in a Roman culture and wrote in a language that predated Spanish.

While most of the poets here are represented by only one or two poems, almost all of them wrote many more. Discussing his reading habits and how he broadened his awareness of fellow bards, Robert Frost remarked: "One of my points of departure is an anthology. I find a poet I admire, and I think, well, there must be a lot to that. Some old one—Shirley, for instance, 'The glories of our blood and state'—that sort of splendid poem. I go looking for more."[1] I hope readers will go looking for more splendid works by the poets they discover here: among them

---

[1] *The Paris Review Interviews: Writers at Work*. Second Series. Edited by George Plimpton. New York: Penguin, 1979. 18.

Yosa Buson, Gyorgy Petri, and Gustavo Adolfo Becquer or even by the better-known Li Po, Anna Akhmatova, and William Carlos Williams.

I particularly wish to thank the translators George Gomori, Dorothy Belle Pollack, Ekaterina Rogalskaya, Karen Van Dyck, John Wilson, and Clive Wilmer for their permission to include their work.

—*Bob Blaisdell*

Contents

Acknowledgments

Anacreon: "Ball Game" by Anacreon, from "Three Translations from the Greek" by Mary Barnard, *Collected Poems*, Breitenbush Books, Portland, OR 1979. Reprinted with permission.

Anonymous: "The nightingale on the flowering plum" by Anonymous. By Kenneth Rexroth, from *In Defense of the Earth*, copyright © 1956 by New Directions Publishing Corp. Reprinted by permission of New Directions Publishing Corp.

Robert Creeley: "I Know a Man" by Robert Creeley, from *Selected Poems*, © 1945 by University of California Press. Reprinted with the permission of the publisher.

Jehudah Halevi: "Ophra," reprinted from *Selected Poems* by Jehudah Halevi, edited by Nina Salaman, by permission of the University of Nebraska Press. Copyright © 1925 by the Jewish Publication Society. Copyright renewed 1956 by the Jewish Publication Society.

Nazim Hikmet: "I Love You," "Optimistic Man," and "After Release From Prison" by Nazim Hikmet from *Poems of Nazim Hikmet*, translated by Randy Blasing and Mutlu Konuk, Translation copyright © 1994, 2002 by Randy Blasing and Mutlu Konuk. Reprinted by permission of Persea Books, Inc., New York.

Taylor Mali: "Because My Students Asked Me" by Taylor Mali from *What Learning Leaves*, Newtown, Connecticut: Hanover Press, Ltd., 2002. Reprinted by permission of the author.

Czeslaw Milosz: "Gift" from *New and Collected Poems: 1931–2001* by Czeslaw Milosz. Copyright © 1988, 1991, 1995, 2001 by Czeslaw Milosz Royalties, Inc. Reprinted by permission of HarperCollins Publishers.

Li Po: "Still Night Thoughts," "A Night with a Friend," and "Autumn Cove" by Li Po from *The Columbia Book of Chinese Poetry: From Early Times to the Thirteenth Century* by Burton Watson. Copyright © 1984 by Columbia University Press. Reprinted with the permission of the publisher.

Su Tung-p'o: "Spring Night" by Su Tung-p'o from *The Columbia Book of Chinese Poetry: From Early Times to the Thirteenth Century* by Burton Watson. Copyright © 1984 by Columbia University Press. Reprinted with the permission of the publisher.

Wang Wei: "Deer Fence" and "Duckweed Pond" by Wang Wei from *The Columbia Book of Chinese Poetry: From Early Times to the Thirteenth Century* by Burton Watson. Copyright © 1984 by Columbia University Press. Reprinted with the permission of the publisher.

Mei Yao-ch'en: "At Night, Hearing Someone Sing in the House Next Door" by Mei Yao-ch'en from *The Columbia Book of Chinese Poetry: From Early Times to the Thirteenth Century* by Burton Watson. Copyright © 1984 by Columbia University Press. Reprinted with the permission of the publisher.

Great
SHORT
POEMS
from
Around the World

Abu'l-Ala al-Ma'rri
(Syria, 973–1058)

"Thus they have passed..."

Thus they have passed, and we shall follow soon
    Into an endless Midnight or a Noon;
The Stars, that likewise oft shoot from their spheres,
    Fall in the arms of wooing Sun or Moon.

—translated from the Arabic by Ameen F. Rihani

Yamabe Akahito
(Japan, d. c. 736)

"Like the mists that ever rise"

Like the mists that ever rise
Over Asuka's quiet pools,
My longing is such
As will not easily die.

—translated from the Japanese by the Iwanami Shoten

1

Anna Akhmatova
(Russia, 1889–1966)

"One can never mistake true tenderness"

One can never mistake true tenderness
  Its touch is serene and sure.
There's no use in your rapt attentiveness,
  Enfolding my shoulders in furs.
And in vain do you speak, submissively
  Words of first, unrequited love.
Well I know what your looks are explicitly
  And insatiably speaking of.

—translated from the Russian by Ekaterina Rogalskaya

The Muse

When, at night, I await
Her, life it seems hangs
  By a hair: glory, youth, freedom —
Laid out before the divine guest
    Pipe in hand.

And here she came! Throwing
Back her veil, carefully she studied me.
  I say to her: "It's *you* who
Dictated to Dante *The Inferno*?"
    She answers: "It is I."

—translated from the Russian by Bob Blaisdell

Richard Aldington
(England, 1892–1962)

Evening

The chimneys, rank on rank,
Cut the clear sky;
The moon
With a rag of gauze about her loins
Poses among them, an awkward Venus—

And here am I looking wantonly at her
Over the kitchen sink.

The River

I.

I drifted along the river
    Until I moored my boat
    By these crossed trunks.

Here the mist moves
    Over fragile leaves and rushes,
    Colourless waters and brown fading hills.

She has come from beneath the trees,
    Moving within the mists,
    A floating leaf.

II.

O blue flower of the evening,
    You have touched my face
    With your leaves of silver.

Love me for I must depart.

Amalfi

We will come down to you,
O very deep sea,
And drift upon your pale green waves
Like scattered petals.

We will come down to you from the hills,
From the scented lemon-groves,
From the hot sun.
We will come down,
O Thalassa,
And drift upon
Your pale green waves
Like petals.

Thomas Bailey Aldrich
(U.S.A., 1836–1906)

Memory

My mind lets go a thousand things,
Like dates of wars and deaths of kings
And yet recalls the very hour —
'Twas noon by yonder village tower,
And on the last blue noon in May —
The wind came briskly up this way,
Crisping the brook beside the road;
Then, pausing here, set down its load
Of pine-scents, and shook listlessly
Two petals from that wild-rose tree.

William Allingham
(Ireland, 1824–1889)

Four Ducks on a Pond

Four ducks on a pond,
    A grass-bank beyond,
    A blue sky of spring,
    White clouds on the wing;

What a little thing
    To remember for years —
    To remember with tears!

Alpheius of Mytilene
(Greece, c. 1st century?)

"Unhappy they whose life is loveless"

Unhappy they whose life is loveless;
    for without love
        it is not easy to do aught or to say aught.

I, for example, am now all too slow,
    but were I to catch sight of Xenophilus
        I would fly swifter than lightning.

Therefore I bid all men not to shun
    but to pursue sweet desire;
        Love is the whetstone of the soul.

—*translated from* The Greek Anthology *by W. R. Paton*

Anacreon
(Greece, 582 B.C.–485 B.C.)

Nature's Laws

Earth drinks up brook,
    And then the tree
Drinks up the earth.
    In turn the sea
Drinks rivers up.
    And so 'tis done.
Sun drinks up sea,
    And moon the sun.
Well then, my friends,
    Don't make outcry;
If all do drink,
    Why shouldn't I?

—translated from the Greek by Dorothy Belle Pollack

Ball Game

Golden haired Love
calls me (tossing
me his bright ball)

to come and play at
catch with a young
thing in red sandals.

But she, being off
prosperous Lesbos,
finds fault with my

gray hairs: she hangs
around open-mouthed
after another man.

—translated from the Greek by Mary Barnard

❦

Anonymous
(Greece, 1st century–6th century)

"The way down to Hades"

> The way down to
> Hades
> is
> straight,
> whether you
> start from Athens or
> whether you betake
> yourself there,
> when dead,
> from Meroe.

> Let it not vex thee
> to die
> far from thy
> country.
> One fair wind
> to
> Hades
> blows
> from all
> lands.

—translated from The Greek Anthology *by W. R. Paton*

"Young Men dancing, and the old"

Young Men dancing, and the old
    Sporting I wish joy behold;
But an old Man gay and free
    Dancing most I love to see:
Age and youth alike he shares,
    For his Heart belies his Hairs.

—*translated from* The Greek Anthology
    by Thomas Stanley

"Caught, Thrasybulus, in the net of a boy's love"

Caught, Thrasybulus,
            in the net of a boy's love,
thou gaspest like a dolphin on the beach,
            longing for the waves,
and not even Perseus' sickle is sharp enough
    to cut through
            the net that binds thee.

—*translated from* The Greek Anthology *by W. R. Paton*

"The love of women touches not my heart"

The love of women touches not my heart,
    but male brands have heaped
        unquenchable coals of fire on me.

Greater is this heat:
    by as much as a man is stronger than a woman,
        by so much is this desire sharper.

—*translated from* The Greek Anthology *by W. R. Paton*

"Persistent Love"

Persistent Love,
    thou ever whirlest at me
            no desire for woman,
    but the lightning of burning
longing for males.

Now burnt by Damon,
    now looking on Ismenus,
I ever suffer long pain.

And not only on these have I looked,
    but my eye,
        ever madly
            roving,
                is dragged into
            the nets
    of all
alike.

—translated from The Greek Anthology *by W. R. Paton*

"My name—my country—what are they to thee?"

My name—my country—what are they to thee?
    What, whether base or proud, my pedigree?
Perhaps I far surpass'd all other men—
    Perhaps I fell below them all—what then?
Suffice it, stranger! that thou seest a tomb:
    Thou know'st its use—it hides—no matter whom.

—translated from The Greek Anthology *by William Cowper*

"Poor in my youth, and in life's later scenes"

Poor in my youth, and in life's later scenes
    Rich to no end, I curse my natal hour,
Who nought enjoy'd, while young, denied the means;
    And nought when old, enjoy'd, denied the power.

—translated from The Greek Anthology *by William Cowper*

Anonymous
(Ireland, c. 7th century)

The Scribe: "A Hedge of Trees"

A hedge of trees surrounds me,
A blackbird's lay sings to me;
    Above my lined booklet
    The trilling birds chant to me.

In a grey mantle from the top of bushes
The cuckoo sings:
    Verily—may the Lord shield me!—
    Well do I write under the greenwood.

—translated from the Irish by Kuno Meyer

Anonymous
(Japan, c. 736)

"As the moon sinks on the mountain-edge"

As the moon sinks on the mountain-edge
The fishermen's lights flicker
    Far out on the dark wide sea.

When we think that we alone
Are steering our ships at midnight,
We hear the splash of oars
        Far beyond us.

—translated from the Japanese by the Iwanami Shoten

Anonymous
(Japan, 8th century)

"The cloud clings"

The cloud clings
        To the high mountain peak—
So would I cling to you, were I a cloud,
        And you, a mountain peak!

—translated from the Japanese by the Iwanami Shoten

Anonymous
(Japan, 8th century)

"While with my sleeves I sweep the bed"

While with my sleeves I sweep the bed
    And sit up, lonely, awaiting you,
The moon has sunk.

—translated from the Japanese by the Iwanami Shoten

Anonymous
(Japan, 8th–10th centuries)

"The nightingale on the flowering plum"

The nightingale on the flowering plum
    The stag beneath the autumn maple.
        And you and me together in bed,
Happy as two fish in the water.

—translated from the Japanese by Kenneth Rexroth

Anonymous
(Japan, c. 900)

Moonlight

    Moonlight in vast
   space is so cold the
    water its beams
      reach first
     freezes first

—translated from the Japanese by John Wilson

Anonymous
(Ireland, 9th century)

Three Triads

The rudest three of all the sons of earth:
A youngster of an old man making mirth,
A strong man at a sick man poking fun,
A wise man gibing at a foolish one.

Three signs that show a fop; the comb-track in his hair,
The track of his nice teeth upon his nibbled fare.
His cane track in the dust, oft as he takes the air.

Three keys that most unlock our secret thinking
Are love and trustfulness and overdrinking.

—translated from the Irish by Alfred Perceval Graves

Anonymous
(Persia, 10th century)

"Ah, would that I could hide within my songs"

Ah, would that I could hide within my songs
    And, every time you sang them, kiss your lips.

—translated from the Persian by Edward Powys Mathers

Anonymous
(Persia, 10th century)

Grief

If grief like fire should give out smoke
    Ever it would be night on earth.

—translated from the Persian by Edward Powys Mathers

Anonymous
(Kafiristan, c. 10th century)

Song

Since you love me and I love you
 The rest matters not;
 I will cut grass in the fields
And you will sell it for beasts.

Since you love me and I love you
 The rest matters not;
 I will sow maize in the fields
And you will sell it for people.

—translated from the Kafir by Edward Powys Mathers

Anonymous
(England, c.1250)

Cuckoo Song

Summer is y-comen in,
 Loudly sing, Cuckoo!
Groweth seed and bloweth mead,
 And springeth wood anew.
  Sing, Cuckoo!

Loweth after calf the cow,
 Bleatheth after lamb the ewe,
Buck doth gambol, bullock amble,—
 Merry sing, Cuckoo!
 Cuckoo, Cuckoo! Well singest thou
 Cuckoo! nor cease thou ever now.

Sing, Cuckoo now, sing Cuckoo.
Sing, Cuckoo, sing Cuckoo now.

Anonymous
(England, 15th century)

"Adam lay ybounden"

Adam lay ybounden,
   Bounden in a bond;
Four thousand winter
   Thought he not too long.
   And all was for an apple,
   An apple that he took,
As clerkes finden written
   In their book.
Nor the apple taken been,
   The apple taken been,
Then never had our Lady
   A-been heaven's queen.
Blessed be the time
   That apple taken was!
Therefore we may singen
   Deo Gratias!

Anonymous
(Ireland, 13–15th centuries)

Youth and Age

Once I was yellow-haired, and ringlets fell
In clusters round my brow;

Grizzled and sparse tonight my short grey crop,
   No luster in it now.

Better to me the shining locks of youth,
Or raven's dusky hue,
Than dear old age, which chilly wisdom brings,
   If what they say be true.

I only know that as I pass the road
No woman looks my way;
They think my head and heart alike are cold—
   Yet I have had my day.

—translated from the Irish by Eleanor Hull

Anonymous
(Germany, 15th century)

Westphalian Song

When thou to my true-love com'st
Greet her from me kindly;
When she asks thee how I fare?
   Say, folks in Heaven fare finely.

When she asks, "What! Is he sick?"
Say, dead!—and when for sorrow
She begins to sob and cry,
   Say, I come tomorrow.

—translated from the German by Samuel Taylor Coleridge

Anonymous
(England, 15th–16th century)

"Western wind, when wilt thou blow?"

Western wind, when wilt thou blow?
That the small rain down can rain.
Christ, that my love were in my arms,
 And I in my bed again!

Anonymous
(Persia, c. 16th century)

"Give justice, O blue sky"

Give justice, O blue sky,
 Which of these two walked more beautifully;
 Either thy world-illuminating sun from the side of
  Morn,
 Or my world-traversing moon from the side of Eve.

—translated from the Persian by Muhammad Abdul Ghani

Anonymous
(England, 16th–17th century)

"O sleep, fond Fancy, sleep, my head thou tirest"

O sleep, fond Fancy, sleep, my head thou tirest
 With false delight of that which thou desirest.
Sleep, sleep, I say, and leave my thoughts molesting,
 Thy master's head hath need of sleep and resting.

Anonymous
(England, 17th century)

Madrigal ("My Love in her attire doth shew her wit")

My Love in her attire doth shew her wit,
　　It doth so well become her;
For every season she hath dressings fit,
　　For Winter, Spring, and Summer.
No beauty she doth miss,
When all her robes are on:
But Beauty's self she is
　　When all her robes are gone.

Anonymous
(Japan, 18th century)

"I see the snowy winter sky"

I see the snowy winter sky
　　through the old arch;
And in the middle the line of
　　one tree.
A flight of crows comes just
　　above the tree,
Sweeping to left and right,
　　and tailing out behind.
　　I think of you.

—translated from the Japanese by Edward Powys Mathers

Anonymous
(Pima, North America, 19th century)

Quail Song

The grey quails bunched tight together.
  Above, Coyote trotted by.
    He stopped. He looked.

The blue quails ran and huddled together.
  Coyote looked at them,
    sideways.

Anonymous
(Navajo, North America, 19th century)

Magpie Song

The magpie! The magpie! Here underneath
In the white of his wings are the footsteps of morning.
     It dawns! It dawns!

—translated from the Navajo by Washington Matthews

Anonymous
(Afganistan, 19th century)

Black Hair

Last night my kisses
  drowned in the softness of black hair,
And my kisses like bees
    went plundering the softness of black hair.

Last night my hands were thrust
  in the mystery of black hair,
And my kisses like bees went plundering
    the sweetness of pomegranates

And among the scents of the harvest
  above my queen's neck, the harvest of black hair;
And my teeth played with the golden skin of her two ears.

Last night my kisses drowned
  in the softness of black hair,
And my kisses like bees
    went plundering the softness of black hair.

—translated from the Afghan of Muhammadji
  by Edward Powys Mathers

Anonymous
(Chippewa, North America, 20th century)

Spring Song

As my eyes search the prairie
  I feel the summer in the spring.

—translated from the Chippewa by Frances Densmore

Song of the Trees

The wind
    Only
I am afraid of.

—translated from the Chippewa by Frances Densmore

The Approach of the Storm

From the half
   Of the sky
   That which lives there
Is coming, and makes a noise.

—*translated from the Chippewa by Frances Densmore*

A Loon I Thought It Was

A loon I thought it was,
   But it was my love's splashing oar.

The Sault Ste. Marie he has departed,
My love has gone on before me,
   Never again can I see him.

A loon I thought it was,
   But it was my love's splashing oar.

—*translated from the Chippewa by Frances Densmore*

Anonymous
(Burma, 20th century)

Envoy

The night before last night
I heard that to make songs to girls
And to make prayers to God
Were of equal value
In the eyes of time:

Provided, that is,
That the prayers
Are sufficiently beautiful.

—translated from the Burmese by Edward Powys Mathers

Anonymous
(Acoman, North America, 20th century)

Butterfly Song

Butterfly, butterfly, butterfly, butterfly,
    Oh, look, see it hovering among the flowers,
It is like a baby trying to walk and not knowing how to go.
    The clouds sprinkle down the sun.

—translated from the Acoman by Frances Densmore

Anonymous
(Inuit, North America, 20th century)

Ptarmigan

A small ptarmigan sat
    in the middle of the plain
    on top of a snowdrift.
Its eyelids were red
  and its back streaked brown.
And right under its cute tail feathers
    sat the sweetest little rump.

Anonymous
(Teton Sioux, North America, 20th century)

You Have No Horses

Well,
when I was courting
"horses you have none"
To me was said.

Therefore, over the land
I roam.

—translated from the Sioux by Frances Densmore

Anonymous
(Wintu, North America, 20th century)

Minnow and Flowers

flowers droop
flowers rise back up
above
the place where
the minnow sleeps while
her fins move slowly
back & forward
forward
&
back

Anonymous
(Greece, 20th century)

"I took up my lament"

I took up my lament
screaming like a crazy woman:
God is a criminal
for killing my son!

My friends and neighbors
tell me not to curse God.
They say that to do so
is sinful and wrong.

I answer them back:
This thing God did,
this killing my son,
was it not sinful and wrong?

—translated from the Greek by Karen Van Dyck

Anonymous
(Yaqui, North America, 20th century)

Yaqui Song

Many pretty flowers, red, blue and yellow.
   We say to the girls, "Let us go
      and walk among the flowers."
            The wind comes and sways the flowers.
         The girls are like that when they dance.
               Some are wide-open, large flowers, and
   some are tiny little flowers.

The birds love the sunshine and the starlight.

The flowers smell sweet.

The girls are sweeter than the flowers.

Anonymous
(Osage, North America, 20th century)

The Rising of the Buffalo Men

I rise, I rise,
I, whose tread makes the earth to rumble.

I rise, I rise,
I, in whose thighs there is strength.

I rise, I rise,
I, who whips his back with his tail when in rage.

I rise, I rise,
I, in whose humped shoulder there is power.

I rise, I rise,
I, who shakes his mane when angered.

I rise, I rise,
I, whose horns are sharp and curved.

—*translated from the Osage by Francis La Flesche*

Asclepiades

(Greece, 3rd century B.C.)

"Thou hoardest still thy maidenhead's hid treasure"

Thou hoardest still thy maidenhead's hid treasure,
    And yet what profit hast thou of thy care?
    For down in Hades, girl, there is no pleasure
Nor wilt thou find a faithful lover there.

The joys of Cypris are among the living,
    And when to awful Acheron we go,
    We shall have nothing, maiden, of her giving,
But dust and ashes all shall lie below.

—*translated from the Greek by Jane Minot Sedgwick*

"Sweet to the thirsty"

Sweet to the thirsty the draught that is cooled with
        snow in the summer;
    Sweet, at the sailor's return, flowering garlands of
        spring,
After the winter is over; but sweetest of all when two
        lovers
    Sheltered under one cloak, both tell their tale of
        true love.

—*translated from the Greek by Jane Minot Sedgwick*

Matsuo Basho
(Japan, 1644–1694)

"The quiet pond"

> The quiet pond
> A frog leaps in
> The sound of water

—translated from the Japanese by Edward G. Seidensticker

"Sleeping at noon"

> sleeping at noon
> the body of the blue heron
> poised in nobility

—translated from the Japanese by Earl Miner

"The roadside thistle"

> The roadside thistle, eager
> To see the travelers pass,
> Was eaten by the passing ass!

—translated from the Japanese by Curtis Hidden Page

"Will you turn toward me?"

> Will you turn toward me?
> I am lonely too,
> this autumn evening

—translated from the Japanese by Makoto Ueda

Charles Baudelaire
(France, 1821–1867)

The Voyage

Oh Death, old captain, raise anchor; 'tis dark.
This life here but bores us. Oh Death, now embark!
Black as ink are the sky and the sea below,
But the rays of light fill our hearts; this you know.

Oh, pour forth your poison, to soothe! We desire
(So much is our brain inflamed by this fire)
To plunge to the depths of the gulf, hear the knell.
For what does it matter—Heaven or hell—
If only the vast unknown we may view,
There to find something new, something new!

—translated from the French by Dorothy Belle Pollack

Gustavo Adolfo Bécquer
(Spain, 1836–1870)

Rhyme 10

The invisible particles of the air
   Quiver and ignite around me;
   The sky dissolves into rays of gold;
   The earth shudders with joy;
I hear the murmur of kisses and the beating of wings
Floating on waves of harmony;
   My eyelids close ... What can it be?
      —It is love passing by!

—translated from the Spanish by Eugenio Florit

Rhyme 21

"What is poetry?" you ask, while you fix
    your blue eyes on my eyes.
What is poetry?! And *you* ask me that?
    Poetry…is you.

—*translated from the Spanish by Stanley Appelbaum*

Rhyme 30

A tear appeared in her eyes,
    and an expression of forgiveness on my lips.
Pride spoke and her tears dried
    and the phrase died away on my lips.

I am journeying down one road; she, down another;
    but when I think about the love we shared
I still say: "Why did I keep silent that day?"
    And she must be saying, "Why didn't I weep?"

—*translated from the Spanish by Stanley Appelbaum*

Rhyme 38

Sighs are air, and go to the air.
    Tears are water, and to the sea flow.
Tell me, woman: when love's forgot,
    Knowest where it doth go?

—*translated from the Spanish by Young Allison*

Rhyme 50

Just as a savage with awkward hands
    fashions a god from a log as the fancy takes him
    and then kneels before his own handiwork:
that's how you and I behaved.

We gave a real shape to a specter
    that was a laughable invention of our mind,
    and once the idol was fashioned, we sacrificed
our love at its altar.

    —translated from the Spanish by Stanley Appelbaum

Bhartrihari
(India, c. 500 A.D.)

"The silvery laughter; eyes that sparkle bold"

The silvery laughter; eyes that sparkle bold,
    Or droop in virgin rue;
    The prattling words of wonder uncontrolled
When world and life are new;

The startled flight and dallying slow return,
    And all their girlish sport;—
    Ah me, that they time's ruinous truth must learn,
Their flowering be so short!

    —translated from the Sanskrit by Paul Elmer More

"Brightly the hearth-fire leap, and the lit lamp"

Brightly the hearth-fire leap, and the lit lamp
Be burning clear and high;

Let sun or moon and starry hosts encamp
   With beacons in the sky: —

Yet darkness in my heart and all is dark,
   Till I behold thine eyes and their love-spark.

—translated from the Sanskrit by Paul Elmer More

"But to remember her my heart is sad"

But to remember her my heart is sad,
          To see her is to know
Bewildered thoughts, and touching driveth mad,
          How is she dear that worketh only woe?

—translated from the Sanskrit by Paul Elmer More

"The sportive Love-god in this worldly sea"

The sportive Love-god in this worldly sea
Angles continually;
And women are his hook, their luring lips
          The bait that bobs and dips.
We greedy fools, like silly nibbling fish,
          Are landed with a swish;
And then, alack! to end the cruel game
          Are broiled on love's
              quick flame.

—translated from the Sanskrit by Paul Elmer More

Bhaſa
(India, c. 300 A.D.)

The Moon

When its rays fall on its cheeks the cat licks them,
    thinking them milk;
  When they are caught in the cleft of a tree the
    elephant deems them a lotus;
When they rest on the couch of lovers the maiden seizes
    them, saying, "'Tis my robe";
  The moon in truth, proud of its brilliance, doth lead
    astray all this world.

—translated from the Sanskrit by Arthur Berriedale Keith

Elizabeth Biſhop
(U.S.A., 1911–1979)

Song

Summer is over upon the sea.
The pleasure yacht, the social being,
that danced on the endless polished floor,
stepped and side-stepped like Fred Astaire,
is gone, is gone, docked somewhere ashore.

The friends have left, the sea is bare
that was strewn with floating, fresh green weeds.
Only the rusty-sided freighters
go past the moon's marketless craters
and the stars are the only ships of pleasure.

William Blake
(England, 1757–1827)

The Fly

Little Fly,
Thy summer's play
My thoughtless hand
Has brushed away.

Am not I
A fly like thee?
Or art not thou
A man like me?

For I dance
And drink, and sing,
Till some blind hand
Shall brush my wing.

If thought is life
And strength and breath
And the want
Of thought is death;

Then am I
A happy fly,
If I live,
Or if I die.

Bertolt Brecht
(Germany, 1898–1956)

The Mask of Evil

On my walls hangs a Japanese carving,
The mask of an evil demon, decorated with gold lacquer.
Sympathetically I observe
The swollen veins of the forehead, indicating
What a strain it is to be evil.

—translated from the German by H. R. Hays

Emily Brontë
(England, 1818–1848)

"The night is darkening round me"

The night is darkening round me,
The wild winds coldly blow;
But a tyrant spell has bound me,
And I cannot, cannot go.

The giant trees are bending
Their bare boughs weighed with snow;
The storm is fast descending,
And yet I cannot go.

Clouds beyond clouds above me,
Wastes beyond wastes below;
But nothing drear can move me;
I will not, cannot go.

Robert Browning
(England, 1812–1889)

Bad Dreams

Last night I saw you in my sleep:
And how your charm of face was changed!
I asked, "Some love, some faith you keep?"
You answered, "Faith gone, love estranged."

Whereat I woke, a twofold bliss:
Waking was one, but next there came
This other: "Though I felt, for this,
My heart break, I loved on the same."

Pippa's Song

The year's at the spring,
And day's at the morn;
Morning's at seven;
The hill-side's dew-pearl'd;
The lark's on the wing;
The snail's on the thorn;
God's in his heaven—
All's right with the world!

Yosa Buson
(Japan, 1716–1783)

"Struck…"

> struck by a
> raindrop, snail
> closes up.

—translated from the Japanese by Janine Beichman

Lord Byron, George Gordon
(England, 1788–1824)

"So, we'll no more go a roving"

So, we'll no more go a roving
So late into the night,
Though the heart be still as loving,
And the moon be still as bright.

For the sword outwears its sheath,
And the soul wears out the breast,
And the heart must pause to breathe,
And Love itself have rest.

Though the night was made for loving,
And the day returns too soon,
Yet we'll go no more a roving
By the light of the moon.

Callimachos
(Greece, 310–c.240 B.C.)

Elegy for Heraclitus

They told me, Heraclitus, thou wert dead,
    And then I thought, and tears thereon did shed,
How oft we two talked down the sun;
    But thou Halicarnassian guest! art ashes now.
Yet live thy nightingales of song: on those
    Forgetfulness her hand shall ne'er impose.

—translated from the Greek by H. N. Coleridge

Joseph Campbell
(Ireland, 1879–1944)

The Old Woman

As a white candle
    In a holy place,
        So is the beauty
            Of an aged face.

As the spent radiance
    Of the winter sun,
        So is a woman
            With her travail done.

Her brood gone from her
    And her thoughts as still
        As the waters
            Under a ruined mill.

The Hills of Cualann

In the youth of summer
The hills of Cualann
Are two golden horns,
Two breasts of childing,
Two tents of light

In the ancient winter
They are two rusted swords,
Two waves of darkness
Two moons of ice.

&

Thomas Campion
(England, 1567–1620)

"When to her lute Corinna sings"

When to her lute Corinna sings,
   Her voice revives the leaden strings,
And doth in highest notes appear
   As any challenged echo clear;
But when she doth of mourning speak,
   Ev'n with her sighs the strings do break.

And as her lute doth live or die,
   Let by her passion, so must I:
For when of pleasure she doth sing,
   My thoughts enjoy a sudden spring,
But if she doth of sorrow speak,
   Ev'n from my heart the strings do break.

"Though you are young and I am old"

Though you are young and I am old,
Though your veins hot, and my blood cold,
Though youth is moist, and age is dry,
Yet embers live, when flames doe die.

The tender graft is easily broke,
But who shall shake the sturdy oak?
You are more fresh and faire than I,
Yet stubs do live when flowers do die.

Thou that thy youth doest vainly boast,
Know buds are soonest nipt with frost,
Think that thy fortune still doth cry,
Thou fool, tomorrow thou must die.

Catullus
(Rome, c. 82 B.C.–c. 54 B.C.)

"Thou saidst that I alone thy Heart could move"

Thou saidst that I alone thy Heart could move,
   And that for me thou wouldst abandon Jove.
   I loved thee then, not with a Love defiled,
But as a Father loves his only Child.

I know thee now, and though I fiercelier burn,
   Thou art become the Object of my Scorn.
   See what thy Falsehood gets; I must confess
I love thee more, but I esteem thee less.

—translated from the Latin by William Walsh

"Lesbia for ever on me rails"

Lesbia for ever on me rails,
    To talk of me she never fails.
Now, hang me, but for all her Art,
    I find that I have gain'd her Heart.
My proof is thus: I plainly see,
    The Case is just the same with me;
I curse her ev'ry hour sincerely,
    Yet, hang me, but I love her dearly.

—*translated from the Latin by Jonathan Swift*

Gutierre de Cetina
(Spain, 1520–1560)

Madrigal

Bright and serene eyes,
    If you are praised for having a sweet glance,
Why when looking at me do you look angrily?

If the kinder you are
    The more beautiful you seem to him who gazes at you,
    Do not look at me in anger
So as not to appear less beautiful.

Oh, raging torments!
    Bright and serene eyes,
Even though you look at me thus, at least do look at me.

—*translated from the Spanish by Eugenio Florit*

Wang Chi
(China, 584–644)

Tell Me Now

"Tell me now, what should a man want
But to sit alone, sipping his cup of wine?"

I should like to have visitors come and discuss philosophy
    And not to have the tax-collector coming to collect
        taxes;
    My three sons married into good families
    And my five daughters wedded to steady husbands.
Then I could jog through a happy five-score years
And, at the end, need no Paradise.

—translated from the Chinese by Arthur Waley

T'ao Ch'ien
(China, 372–427)

"A long time ago"

A long time ago
        I went on a journey,
        Right to the corner
        Of the Eastern Ocean.

The road there
        Was long and winding,
        And stormy waves
        Barred my path.
        What made me
        Go this way?

Hunger drove me
    Into the World.

I tried hard
    To fill my belly,
    And even a little
    Seemed a lot.

But this was clearly
    A bad bargain,
    So I went home
    And lived in idleness.

—translated from the Chinese by Arthur Waley

Po Chu-i
(China, 772–846)

Resignation

Keep off your thoughts from things that are past and done;
    For thinking of the past wakes regret and pain.

Keep off your thoughts from thinking what will happen;
    To think of the future fills one with dismay.

Better by day to sit like a sack in your chair;
    Better by night to lie like a stone in your bed.

When food comes, then open your mouth;
    When sleep comes, then close your eyes.

—translated from the Chinese by Arthur Waley

Illness

Dear friends, there is no cause for so much sympathy.
   I shall certainly manage from time to time to take my
      walks abroad.

All that matters is an active mind, what is the use of feet?
   By land one can ride in a carrying-chair; by water, be
      rowed in a boat.

—*translated from the Chinese by Arthur Waley*

Matthias Claudius
(Germany, 1740–1815)

Death and the Maiden

THE MAIDEN:
      Go past, oh, go past, you wild skeleton!
      I am still young! Go, dear one, and do not touch me!

DEATH:
      Give me your hand, you beautiful and tender shape!
      I am a friend and do not come to punish.
      Be of good cheer! I am not wild!
      You shall sleep softly in my arms!

—*translated from the German by Gustave Mathieu and*
Guy Stern

Abraham Cowley
(England, 1618–1667)

The Epicure

Fill the bowl with rosy wine,
    Around our temples roses twine,
    And let us cheerfully awhile
Like the wine and roses smile.

Crowned with roses, we contemn
    Gyges' wealthy diadem.
    Today is ours; what do we fear?
Today is ours; we have it here.

Let's treat it kindly, that it may
    Wish, at least, with us to stay.
    Let's banish business, banish sorrow;
To the gods belongs tomorrow.

John Clare
(England, 1793–1864)

The Secret

I loved thee, though I told thee not,
    Right earlily and long,
Thou wert my joy in every spot,
    My theme in every song.

And when I saw a stranger face
    Where beauty held the claim,
I gave it like a secret grace
    The being of thy name.

And all the charms of face or voice
    Which I in others see
Are but the recollected choice
    Of what I felt for thee.

Adelaide Crapsey
(U.S.A., 1878–1914)

November Night

Listen...
With faint dry sound,
Like steps of passing ghosts,
The leaves, frost-crisp'd, break from the trees
And fall.

The Guarded Wound

If it
Were lighter touch
Than petal of flower resting
On grass, oh still too heavy it were,
Too heavy!

On Seeing Weather-Beaten Trees

Is it as plainly in our living shown,
By slant and twist, which way the wind hath blown?

Robert Creeley
(U.S.A., 1926–2005)

I Know a Man

As I sd to my
friend, because I am
always talking, — John, I

sd, which was not his
name, the darkness sur-
rounds us, what

can we do against
it, or else, shall we &
why not, buy a goddamn big car,

drive, he sd, for
christ's sake, look
out where yr going.

Dakiki
(Persia, d. 975)

"O would that in the world there were no night"

O would that in the world there were no night,
    That I might ne'er be parted from her lips!
No scorpion-sting would sink deep in my heart
    But for her scorpion coils of darkest hair.

If 'neath her lip no starry dimple shone,
    I would not linger with the stars till day;

And if she were not cast in beauty's mold,
   My soul would not be molded of her love.

      If I must live without my well-beloved,
      O God! I would there were no life for me.

—*translated from the Persian by Reynold A. Nicholson*

Samuel Daniel
(England, 1562–1619)

"Love is a sickness full of woes"

Love is a sickness full of woes,
   All remedies refusing;
A plant that with most cutting grows,
   Most barren with best using.
      Why so?
More we enjoy it, more it dies;
If not enjoyed, it sighing cries,
      Heigh ho!

Love is a torment of the mind,
   A tempest everlasting;
And Jove hath made it of a kind
   Not well, not full, nor fasting.
      Why so?
More we enjoy it, more it dies;
If not enjoyed, it sighing cries,
      Heigh ho!

Emily Dickinson
(U.S.A., 1830–1886)

"I'm Nobody! Who are you?"

I'm Nobody! Who are you?
Are you–Nobody–too?
Then there's a pair of us?
Don't tell! they'd advertise–you know!

How dreary–to be–Somebody!
How public–like a Frog–
To tell one's name–the livelong June–
To an admiring Bog!

"The Soul selects her own Society"

The Soul selects her own Society—
Then—shuts the Door—
To her divine Majority—
Present no more—

Unmoved—she notes the Chariots—pausing—
At her low Gate—
Unmoved—an Emperor be kneeling
Upon her Mat—

I've known her—from an ample nation—
Choose One—
Then—close the Valves of her attention—
Like Stone—

"There's a certain Slant of light"

There's a certain Slant of light,
Winter Afternoons —
That oppresses, like the Heft
Of Cathedral Tunes —

Heavenly Hurt, it gives us —
We can find no scar,
But internal difference,
Where the Meanings, are —

None may teach it — Any —
'Tis the Seal Despair —
An imperial affliction
Sent us of the air —

When it comes, the Landscape listens —
Shadows — hold their breath —
When it goes, 'tis like the Distance
On the look of Death —

Dilsoz
(India, 18th century)

"If the proud girl I love..."

If the proud girl I love would cast a glance behind her,
  As down the road she swings in her bright palanquin,
She would see her lover on foot,
              with empty hands.

Like the white buds of tuberose in a dark night
   Through the lines of betel
   shine out her white teeth.

When she puts henna on her hands and dives in the soft
   river
  One would think
   one saw fire
    twisting and
    running
    in the
     water.

—translated from the Hindustani by Edward Powys Mathers

Digby Mackworth Dolben
(England, 1848–1867)

Requests

I asked for Peace—
  My sins arose,
  And bound me close,
I could not find release.

I asked for Truth—
  My doubts came in,
  And with their din
They wearied all my youth.

I asked for Love—
  My lovers failed,
  And griefs assailed
Around, beneath, above.

I asked for Thee —
   And thou didst come
   To take me home
Within Thy Heart to be.

H. D. (Hilɒa Doolittle)
(U.S.A., 1886–1961)

Song

You are as gold
as the half-ripe grain
that merges to gold again,
as white as the white rain
that beats through
the half-opened flowers
of the great flower tufts
thick on the black limbs
of an Illyrian apple bough.

Can honey distill such fragrance
As your bright hair —
for your face is as fair as rain,
yet as rain that lies clear
on white honey-comb,
lends radiance to the white wax,
so your hair on your brow
casts light for a shadow.

Paul Laurence Dunbar
(U.S.A., 1872–1906)

Silence

'Tis better to sit here beside the sea,
   Here on the spray-kissed beach,
in silence, that between such friends as we
   Is full of deepest speech.

Compensation

Because I had loved so deeply,
   Because I had loved so long,
God in His great compassion
   Gave me the gift of song.

Because I have loved so vainly,
   And sung with such faltering breath,
The Master in infinite mercy
   Offers the boon of Death.

Theology

There is a heaven, for ever, day by day,
The upward longing of my soul doth tell me so.
There is a hell, I'm quite as sure; for pray,
If there were not, where would my neighbors go?

T. S. Eliot
(U.S.A./England, 1888–1965)

Morning at the Window

They are rattling breakfast plates in basement kitchens,
And along the trampled edges of the street
I am aware of the damp souls of housemaids
Sprouting despondently at area gates.

The brown waves of fog toss up to me
Twisted faces from the bottom of the street,
And tear from a passer-by with muddy skirts
An aimless smile that hovers in the air
And vanishes along the level of the roofs.

Juan Escriva
(Spain, 15th century)

Welcome Death

Come, gentle death! come silently, —
    And sound no knell, no warning give,
Lest the sweet bliss of welcoming thee
    Should rouse my wearied soul to live.

Come like the rapid lightning's ray,
    That wounds, but while it wounds is still;
It passes, voiceless, on its way,
    And flings its mortal barb at will.
Thus soft, thus calm, thy coming be,
    Else, death! this warning now I give,

That the sweet bliss of welcoming thee
 Will rouse my weary soul to live.

—translated from the Spanish by John Bowring

Euenus
(Greece, 1st century B.C.)

The Vine to the Goat

Although you eat me to the root,
 I yet shall bear enough of fruit
For wine to sprinkle your dim eyes,
 When you are made a sacrifice.

—translated from the Greek by Henry Van Dyke

Firdawsi
(Persia, 935–1025)

Reproach

Were it mine to repose for one night on thy bosom,
 My head, thus exalted, would reach to the skies;
In Mercury's fingers the pen I would shatter;
 The crown of the Sun I would grasp as my prize.
O'er the ninth sphere of heaven my soul would be flying
 And Saturn's proud head 'neath my feet would be lying,
Yet I'd pity poor lovers sore wounded and dying,
 Were thy beauty mine own, or thy lips, or thine eyes.

—translated from the Persian by Edward G. Browne

❧

John Gould Fletcher
(U.S.A., 1886–1950)

Kurenai-ye (or "Red Picture")

She glances expectantly
   Through the pine avenue,
   To the cherry-tree summit
Where her lover will appear.

Paint rose anticipation colors her,
   And sunset;
She is a cherry-tree that has taken long to bloom.

Memory and Forgetting

I have forgotten how many times he kissed me,
   But I cannot forget
   A swaying branch—a leaf that fell
To earth.

Changing Love

My love for her at first was like the smoke that drifts
   Across the marshes
From burning woods.

But, after she had gone,
   It was like the lotus that lifts up
Its heart shaped buds from the dim waters.

Fugitive Beauty

As the fish that leaps from the river,
    As the dropping of a November leaf at twilight,
    As the faint flicker of lightning down the southern
sky, So I saw beauty, far away.

F. S. Flint
(England, 1885–1960)

Cones

The blue mist of after-rain
    fills all the trees;

The sunlight gilds the tops
    of the poplar spires, far off,
    behind the houses.

Here a branch sways
    and there
        a sparrow twitters.

The curtain's hem, rose-embroidered,
    flutters, and half reveals
    a burnt-red chimney pot.

The quiet in the room
    bears patiently
    a footfall on the street.

Terror

Eyes are tired;
   the lamp burns,
   and in its circle of light
   papers and books lie
   where chance and life
   have placed them.

Silence sings all around me;
   my head is bound with a band;
   outside in the street a few footsteps;
   a clock strikes the hour.

I gaze, and my eyes close,
   slowly:

I doze; but the moment before sleep,
   a voice calls my name
   in my ear,
   and the shock jolts my heart:
   but when I open my eyes,
   and look, first left, and then right...

no one is there.

Robert Frost
(U.S.A., 1874–1963)

Fire and Ice

Some say the world will end in fire,
Some say in ice.
From what I've tasted of desire

I hold with those who favor fire.
But if it had to perish twice,
I think I know enough of hate
To say that for destruction ice
Is also great
And would suffice.

Nothing Gold Can Stay

Nature's first green is gold,
Her hardest hue to hold.
Her early leaf's a flower;
But only so an hour.
Then leaf subsides to leaf.
So Eden sank to grief,
So dawn goes down to day.
Nothing gold can stay.

Johann Wolfgang von Goethe
(Germany, 1749–1832)

Calm at Sea

Deep calm prevails on the waters,
    the sea reposes without a stir,
    and, in concern, the seaman
    sees a smooth surface all around.
No breeze from any quarter!
    a frightening, deathly calm!
In the immense expanse
                no wave stirs.

—*translated from the German by Stanley Appelbaum*

"All the time a man is sober"

All the time a man is sober,
   he's pleased with inferior things;
   as soon as he's had a drink,
   he knows what's right;
   only, it's all too easy
   to overdo it:
Hafiz, teach me
     how you managed it!

Because my opinion
   is no exaggeration:
   if you can't drink,
   you shouldn't love;
   but you drinkers shouldn't
   feel superior:
if you can't love,
     you shouldn't drink.

—*translated from the German by Stanley Appelbaum*

Wanderer's Night Song

Over all the mountain peaks is peace,
in all the tree tops you feel
   scarcely a breath;

the little birds are silent in the forest.
Just wait, soon
   you too will be at peace.

—*translated from the German by Harry Steinhauer*

Barnabe Googe
(England, 1540–1594)

A Posy

Two lines shall tell the grief that I by love sustain
    I burn, I flame, I freeze, of hell I feel the pain.

Of Money

Give money me, take friendship whoso list,
    For friends are gone, come once adversity,
When money yet remaineth safe in chest,
    That quickly can thee bring from misery;
Fair face show friends when riches do abound;
    Come time of proof, farewell, they must away;
Believe me well, they are not to be found
    If God but send thee once a lowering day.
Gold never starts aside, but in distress,
    Finds ways enough to ease thine heaviness.

Jehudah Halevi
(Spain, 1085–1140)

Ophra

Ophra washeth her garments in the waters
Of my tears, and spreadeth them out in the sunshine of
    her radiance.
She demandeth no water of the fountains, having my
    two eyes;
And no other sunshine than her beauty.

—translated from the Hebrew by Nina Salaman

❧

Thomas Hardy
(England, 1840–1928)

Her Initials

Upon a poet's page I wrote
Of old two letters of her name;
Part seemed she of the effulgent thought
Whence that high singer's rapture came.
—When now I turn the leaf the same
Immortal light illumes the lay
But from the letters of her name
The radiance has died away.

I Look into My Glass

I look into my glass
   And view my wasting skin,
And say, "Would God it came to pass
   My heart had shrunk as thin!"

For then, I, undistrest
   By hearts grown cold to me,
Could lonely wait my endless rest
   With equanimity.

But Time, to make me grieve,
   Part steals, lets part abide;
And shakes this fragile frame at eve
   With throbbings of noontide.

An Upbraiding

Now I am dead you sing to me
    The songs we used to know,
But while I lived you had no wish
    Or care for doing so.

Now I am dead you come to me
    In the moonlight, comfortless;
Ah, what would I have given alive
    To win such tenderness!

When you are dead, and stand to me
    Not differenced, as now,
But like again, will you be cold
    As when we lived, or how?

John Harington
(England, 1561–1612)

The Author to His Wife, of a Woman's Eloquence

My Mall, I mark that when to prove me
    To buy a velvet gown, or some rich border,
Thou call'st me good sweet heart, thou swear'st to love me,
    Thy locks, thy lips, thy looks, speak all in order,
Thou think'st, and right thou think'st, that these do
        move me,
    That all these severally thy suit do further:
But shall I tell thee what most thy suit advances?
    Thy fair smooth words? no, no, thy fair smooth
        haunches.

Comparison of the Sonnet and the Epigram

Once, by mishap, two poets fell a-squaring,
   The sonnet, and our epigram comparing;
And Faustus, having long demur'd upon it,
   Yet, at the last, gave sentence for the sonnet.
Now, for such censure, this his chief defence is,
Their sugared taste best likes his lickerish senses.
      Well, though I grant sugar may please the taste,
      Yet let my verse have salt to make it last.

Heinrich Heine
(Germany, 1797–1856)

"I wish that all my love-songs"

I wish that all my love-songs
   Were flowers bright and rare;
I'd send them to my dearest
   And she might find them fair.

I wish that all my love-songs
   Were kisses that could speak;
I'd send them to my dearest
   To hang about her cheek.

I wish that these, my love-songs,
   Were peas, so firm and fat;
I'd make a nice, rich pea-soup—
   And she would relish that!

—*translated by Louis Untermeyer*

"Your eyes of azure violets"

Your eyes of azure violets,
Your cheeks of roses red,
Your delicate little hand
With lilies white outspread—
All blossom on forever,
And only your heart is dead.

—translated from the German by Dorothy Belle Pollack

"Ah, yes, my songs are poisoned"

Ah, yes, my songs are poisoned
How can this but be true,
When, in my bloom of life,
You've given me this rue?
Ah yes, my songs are poisoned;
How can this but be true,
When in my heart nest vipers,
And you, my love, and you.

—translated from the German by Dorothy Belle Pollack

Religion

I have no faith in Heaven
    Of which the preachers write;
Your eyes I do believe in,—
    They are my Heaven's light.

I have no faith in Godhead
    Of which the preachers read;
Your heart I do believe in,—
    No other God I need.

I have no faith in Satan,
    In Hell and Hell's fierce smart;
Your eyes I do believe in, —
    And in your wicked heart.

—*translated from the German by Louis Untermeyer*

"The old dream comes again to me"

The old dream comes again to me:
With May-night stars above,
We two sat under the linden-tree
And swore eternal love.

Again and again we plighted troth,
We chattered, and laughed, and kissed;
To make me well remember my oath
You gave me a bite on the wrist.

O darling with the eyes serene,
And with the teeth so white!
The vows were proper to the scene,
Superfluous was the bite.

—*translated from the German by James Thomson*

"I love this white and slender body"

I love this white and slender body,
    These limbs that answer Love's caresses,
Passionate eyes, and forehead covered
    With heavy waves of thick, black tresses.

You are the very one I've searched for
    In many lands, in every weather.

You are my sort; you understand me;
   As equals we can talk together.

In me you've found the man you care for.
   And, for a while, you'll richly pay me
With kindness, kisses and endearments—
   And then, as usual, you'll betray me.

   —translated from the German by Louis Untermeyer

"From pain, wherein I languish"

From pain, wherein I languish,
   My little songs I utter,
And their rustling wings they flutter
   And bear her my tale of anguish.

They find her heart, but stay not:
   They come again with sighing,
They come again with crying;
   Yet what they have seen they say not.

   —translated from the German by Franklin Johnson

George Herbert
(England, 1593–1633)

The Quiddity

My God, a verse is not a crown,
   No point of honor, or gay suit,
No hawk, or banquet, or renown,
   Nor a good sword, nor yet a lute.

It cannot vault, or dance, or play;
   It never was in France or Spain;
Nor can it entertain the day
   With a great stable or domain.

It is no office, art, or news;
   Nor the Exchange, or busy Hall:
But it is that which, while I use,
   I am with Thee: and Most take all.

Robert Herrick
(England, 1591–1674)

Upon Julia's Clothes

Whenas in silks my Julia goes,
   Then, then, methinks, how sweetly flows
That liquefaction of her clothes.

Next, when I cast mine eyes and see
   That brave vibration each way free;
O how that glittering taketh me!

Her Legs

Fain would I kiss my Julia's dainty leg,
   Which is as white and hairless as an egg.

Upon Some Women

Thou who wilt not love, do this,
   Learn of me what woman is.
Something made of thread and thrum,
   A mere botch of all and some,

Pieces, patches, ropes of hair;
   Inlaid garbage everywhere.
Outside silk and outside lawn;
   Scenes to cheat us neatly drawn.
False in legs, and false in thighs;
   False in breast, teeth, hair, and eyes;
False in head, and false enough;
   Only true in shreds and stuff.

To God, on His Sicknesse

What though my harp and viol be
Both hung upon the willow-tree?

What though my bed be now my grave,
And for my house I darkness have?

What though my healthful days are fled,
And I lie numbered with the dead?

Yet I have hope by thy great power
To spring, though now a wither'd flower.

Hermann Hesse
(Germany, 1877–1962)

"I love women..."

I love women who a thousand years ago
   Were loved by poets and in songs extolled.

I love cities whose empty walls
   Bemoan the ancient royal houses.

I love cities that will rise,
    When no one of today is still alive on earth.

I love women—slender, wonderful,
    Who rest unborn within the womb of time.

Some day they will with their starry-pale
    Beauty equal the beauty of my dreams.

—translated by Gustave Mathieu & Guy Stern

Nazim Hikmet
(Turkey, 1902–1963)

I Love You

I love you
like dipping bread into salt and eating
Like waking up at night with high fever
and drinking water, with the tap in my mouth
Like unwrapping the heavy box from the postman
with no clue what it is
fluttering, happy, doubtful
I love you
like flying over the sea in a plane for the first time
Like something moves inside me
when it gets dark softly in Istanbul
I love you
Like thanking God that we live.

—translated from the Turkish by Randy Blasing and
    Mutlu Konuk

Optimistic Man

as a child he never plucked the wings off flies
he didn't tie tin cans to cats' tails
or lock beetles in matchboxes
or stomp anthills
he grew up
and all those things were done to him
I was at his bedside when he died
he said read me a poem
about the sun and the sea
about nuclear reactors and satellites
about the greatness of humanity

*—translated from the Turkish by Randy Blasing and
    Mutlu Konuk*

After Release from Prison

Awake.
Where are you?
At home.
Still unaccustomed—
awake or sleeping—
to being in your own home.
This is just one more of the stupefactions
of spending thirteen years in a prison.
Who's lying at your side?
Not loneliness, but your wife,
in the peaceful sleep of an angel.
Pregnancy looks good on a woman.
What time is it?
Eight.

That means you're safe until evening.
Because it's the practice of police
Never to raid homes in broad daylight.

—translated by Randy Blasing and Mutlu Konuk

Princess Hirokawa
(Japan, 8th century)

"The sheaves of my love-thoughts"

The sheaves of my love-thoughts
   Would fill seven carts—
Carts huge and heavy-wheeled.
     Such a burden I bear
     Of my own choice.

—translated from the Japanese by the Iwanami Shoten

"I thought there could be"

I thought there could be
No more love left anywhere.
Whence then is come this love,
That has caught me now
And holds me in its grasp.

—translated from the Japanese by the Iwanami Shoten

Friedrich Holderlin
(Germany, 1770–1843)

Socrates and Alcibiades

"Why, holy Socrates, do you pay homage
   To this youth constantly? Do you not know anything
      greater?
      Why do your eyes look upon him
         With love, as upon gods?"

He who has thought most deeply loves what is most vital;
   He who has looked into the world understands lofty
      virtue,
      And wise men often incline
         Toward the beautiful at the last.

—*translated from the German by Stanley Appelbaum*

Langston Hughes
(U.S.A., 1902–1967)

Personal

In an envelope marked:
      PERSONAL
God addressed me a letter.
In an envelope marked:
      PERSONAL
I have given my answer.

Death of an Old Seaman

We buried him high on a windy hill,
But his soul went out to sea.
I know, for I heard, when all was still,
His sea-soul say to me:

Put no tombstone at my head,
For here I do not make my bed.
Strew no flowers on my grave,
I've gone back to the wind and wave.
Do not, do not weep for me,
For I am happy with my sea.

The Negro Speaks of Rivers

I've known rivers:
I've known rivers ancient as the world and older than
    the flow of human blood in human veins.

My soul has grown deep like the rivers.

I bathed in the Euphrates when dawns were young.
I built my hut near the Congo and it lulled me to sleep.

I looked upon the Nile and raised the pyramids above it.
I heard the singing of the Mississippi when Abe Lincoln
    went down to New Orleans, and I've seen its muddy
    bosom turn all golden in the sunset.

I've known rivers:
Ancient, dusky rivers.

My soul has grown deep like the rivers.

❧

T. E. Hulme
(England, 1883–1917)

Autumn

A touch of cold in the Autumn night—
I walked abroad,
And saw the ruddy moon lean over a hedge
Like a red-faced farmer.
I did not stop to speak, but nodded;
And round about were the wistful stars
With white faces like town children.

❧

Kobayashi Issa
(Japan, 1763–1828)

"Hey! Don't swat"

> Hey! Don't swat:
> the fly wrings his hands
> on bended knees

—translated from the Japanese by Faubion Bowers

"Thud-thud"

> Thud-thud
> upon the flowers
> drops the horse
> turd

—translated from the Japanese by Hiroaki Sato

Juan Ramon Jiménez
(Spain, 1881–1958)

Yellow Spring

April was coming, full
Of yellow flowers:
The brook was yellow,
The fence, the hill were yellow,
The children's cemetery,
That orchard where love used to live.

The sun anointed the world in yellow
With its fallen light;
Ah, among the golden lilies,
The warm, the golden water;
The yellow butterflies
Over yellow roses!

Yellow garlands were climbing
The trees; the day
Was a gold-incensed blessing,
In a golden awakening of life.
Among the bones of the dead,
God opened His yellow hands.

—*translated from the Spanish by Eugenio Florit*

Ben Jonson
(England, 1572–1637)

Epitaph on Elizabeth, L. H.

Wouldst thou hear what man can say
    In a little? reader, stay.
Underneath this stone doth lie
    As much beauty as could die;
Which in life did harbor give
    To more virtue than doth live.
If at all she had a fault,
    Leave it buried in this vault.
One name was Elizabeth;
    The other, let it sleep with death:
Fitter, where it died, to tell,
    Than that it lived at all. Farewell!

Why I Write Not of Love

Some act of Love's bound to rehearse,
I thought to bind him in my verse:
Which when he felt, Away, quoth he,
    Can poets hope to fetter me?
It is enough, they once did get
Mars and my mother, in their net:
I wear not these my wings in vain.
    With which he fled me; and again,
Into my rhymes could ne'er be got
By any art: then wonder not,
That since, my numbers are so cold,
    When Love is fled, and I grow cold.

The Hourglass

Consider this small dust, here in the glass,
       By atoms moved:
Could you believe that this the body was
       Of one that loved;
And in his mistress' flame playing like a fly,
Was turned to cinders by her eye:
Yes; and in death, as life unblest,
       To have't exprest,
Even ashes of lovers find no rest.

"Still to be neat, still to be dressed"

Still to be neat, still to be dressed,
As you were going to a feast;
Still to be powder'd, still perfum'd:
Lady, it is to be presum'd,
Though Art's hid causes are not found,
All is not sweet, all is not sound.

Give me a look, give me a face,
That makes simplicity a grace;
Robes loosely flowing, hair as free:
Such sweet neglect more taketh me,
Than all the adulteries of Art;
They strike mine eyes, but not my heart.

On My First Daughter

Here lies, to each her parents' ruth,
   Mary, the daughter of her youth;
Yet all heaven's gifts being heaven's due,
   It makes the father less to rue.

At six months' end she parted hence
    With safety of her innocence;
Whose soul heaven's queen, whose name she bears,
    In comfort of her mother's tears,
Hath placed amongst her virgin-train:
    Where, while that severed doth remain,
This grave partakes the fleshly birth;
    Which cover lightly, gentle earth!

"Swell me a bowl with lusty wine"

Swell me a bowl with lusty wine,
Till I may see the plump Lyaeus swim
            Above the brim:
        I drink, as I would write,
In flowing measure, fill'd with flame and sprite.

Kabir
(India, c. 1440–1518)

"A sore pain troubles me day and night"

A sore pain troubles me day and night, and I cannot sleep;
I long for the meeting with my Beloved, and my father's
    house gives me pleasure no more.
The gates of the sky are opened, the temple is revealed:
I meet my husband, and leave at His feet the offering of
    my body and my mind.

—translated from the Hindi by Rabindranath Tagore

"Within this earthen vessel are bowers and groves"

Within this earthen vessel are bowers and groves, and
    within it is the Creator:
Within this vessel are the seven oceans and the
    unnumbered stars.
The touchstone and the jewel-appraiser are within;
And within this vessel the Eternal soundeth, and the
    spring wells up.
Kabir says: "Listen to me, my friend! My beloved Lord
    is within."

—translated from the Hindi by Rabindranath Tagore

Kasa Kanamura
(Japan, 8th century)

"A sojourner in Mika's plains"

A sojourner in Mika's plains,
I saw you on the road,
A stranger to me like a cloud of heaven:
The words I could not speak to you,
Quite choked my heart.
Yet we two, by the mercy of the gods,
Are now wedded in love and trust,
Lying upon each other's sleeve.
Ah, tonight! Would it were as long
As a hundred autumn nights together!

—translated from the Japanese by the Iwanami Shoten

Empress Kogyoku
(Japan, 594–661)

"From the age of the gods"

From the age of the gods
   Men have been begotten and begetting;
   They overflow this land of ours.
I see them go hither and thither
   Like flights of teal—
     But not you whom I love.

So I yearn each day till the day is over
   And each night till the dawn breaks;
     Sleeplessly I pass this long, long night!

—*translated from the Japanese by the Iwanami Shoten*

Alfred Kreymborg
(U.S.A., 1883–1966)

Clay

I wish
there were thirteen
gods in the sky,
even twelve might achieve it:

Or even
one god
in me:

Alone,
I can't shape
an image of her.

Screen Dance: For Rihani

Its posterior pushing
its long thin body,
 a procession of waves lifting its head—
a green caterpiller:

Its roots digging and drinking,
the sap driving outward and up,
shaking its yellow head—
the mountain top of a tree:

Idling along in the blue,
an easy white holiday,
swimming away towards the rim of the bowl—
a cloud:
Dipping and twirling,
soaring, floating, following after—
a butterfly.

Walter Savage Landor
(England, 1775–1864)

Ianthe

From you, Ianthe, little troubles pass
    Like little ripples down a sunny river;
Your pleasures spring like daisies in the grass,
    Cut down, and up again, as blithe as ever.

Emily Lawless
(Ireland, 1845–1913)

In Spain

Your sky is a hard and a dazzling blue,
Your earth and sands are a dazzling gold,
And gold or blue is the proper hue,
You say for a swordsman bold.

In the land I have left the skies are cold,
The earth is green, the rocks are bare,
Yet the devil may hold all your blue and your gold
Were I only once back there!

D. H. Lawrence
(England, 1885–1930)

Brooding Grief

A yellow leaf from the darkness
Hops like a frog before me.
Why should I start and stand still?

I was watching the woman that bore me
Stretched in the brindled darkness
Of the sick-room, rigid with will
To die: and the quick leaf tore me
Back to this rainy swill
Of leaves and lamps and traffic mingled before me.

Nonentity

The stars that open and shut
Fall on my shallow breast
Like stars on a pool.

The soft wind, blowing cool
Laps little crest after crest
Of ripples across my breast.

And dark grass under my feet
Seems to dabble in me
Like grass in a brook.

Oh, and it is sweet
To be all these things, not to be
Any more myself.

For look,
I am weary of myself!

New Year's Eve

There are only two things now,
The great black night scooped out
And this fire-glow.

This fire-glow, the core,
And we the two ripe pips
That are held in store.

Listen, the darkness rings
As it circulates round our fire.
Take off your things.

Your shoulders, your bruised throat!
Your breasts, your nakedness!
This fiery coat!

As the darkness flickers and dips,
As the firelight falls and leaps
From your feet to your lips!

Luis de Leon
(Spain, c.1528–1591)

On Leaving Prison

Falsehood and hatred here
Held me in this prison pent:
Happy whose life is spent
In learning's humble sphere,
Far from the world malevolent;
He, with poor house and fare,
Communing with God alone,
Doth in the country fair
Dwell solitary, there
By none envied, envying more.

—*translated from the Spanish by Aubrey F. G. Bell*

Mikhail Lermontov
(Russia, 1814–1841)

Gratitude

My thanks for all Thou gavest me through the years:
For passion's secret torments without end,

The poisoned kiss, the bitterness of tears,
The vengeful enemy, the slanderous friend,
The spirit's ardor in the desert spent,
Every deception, every wounding wrong;
My thanks for each dark gift that Thou hast sent;
But heed thou that I need not thank Thee long.

—translated from the Russian by Babette Deutsch

"Land of masters, land of slaves, farewell"

Land of masters, land of slaves, farewell,
Unwashed Russia, it's goodbye I say:
You in your blue uniforms, and you
Who were fashioned only to obey.

From your czars I may hide at last
Once the Caucasus between us rears,
And be safe from those all-seeing eyes
And unheard by those all-hearing ears.

—translated from the Russian by Babette Deutsch

Detlev von Liliencron
(Germany, 1844–1909)

Four in Hand

In front, four horses' nodding heads;
Beside me, a girl's two blonde braids;
Behind us, the groom, with self-important airs;
By the wheels, the sound of barking.

In the villages, the contentment of a becalmed life;
In the fields, busy harrows and plows;
All of this illuminated by the sun
So brightly, so brightly.

—translated from the German by Stanley Appelbaum

Federico Garcia Lorca
(Spain, 1898–1936)

Hour of Stars (1920)

The total silence of the night
on the music-stave
of infinity.

I go out into the street naked,
ripe with lost
poetry.
The blackness, riddled
by the cricket's call,
possesses that dead will-o'-the-wisp
of sound.
That musical light
which the spirit
perceives.

The skeletons of a thousand butterflies
sleep in my enclosure.

There is a crowd of wild young breezes
on the river.

—translated from the Spanish by Stanley Appelbaum

❧

Lucilius
(Greece, 148 B.C.–103 B.C.)

"When Ulysses after twenty years"

When Ulysses after twenty years came safe to his home,
   Argos the dog recognized his appearance when he
      saw him,
But you, Stratophon, after boxing for four hours,
   Have become not only unrecognisable to dogs but to
      the city.
If you will trouble to look at your face in a glass, you
      will say on your oath,
   "I am not Stratophon."

—*translated from* The Greek Anthology *by W. R. Paton*

❧

Lady Maisun
(Arabia, c. 650)

She Scorns Her Husband the Caliph

A tent with rustling breezes cool
Delights me more than palace high,
And more the cloak of simple wool
Than robes in which I learned to sigh.

The crust I ate beside my tent
Was more than this fine bread to me;
The wind's voice where the hill-path went
Was more than tambourine can be.

And more than purr of friendly cat
I love the watch-dog's bark to hear;
And more than any lubbard fat
I love a Bedouin cavalier!

—translated from the Arabic by Reynold A. Nicholson

Taylor Mali
(U.S.A., b. 1965)

Because My Students Asked Me

what i would want them to do
at my funeral, i told them:

write & perform a collective poem
in which each of you says a line
about what i was like as a teacher,
about how i made you reach for stars
until you became them,
about how much you loved
to pretend
you hated me.

*You mean even after you die
you're going to make us do work?*

Jorge Manrique
(Spain, 1440?–1479)

Song

With a painful care,
   Discontent, sorrow and pain,
   I depart, a sad lover,
   Forsaken by all my loves,
By my loves, but not by love.

And my own heart, enemy
    Of what my life desires,
    Neither finds life nor dies,
Nor remains, nor goes with me;
    Without fortune, wretched,
    Without comfort, without favor,
I depart, a sad lover,
    Forsaken by all my loves,
      By my loves, but not by love.

—translated from the Spanish by Eugenio Florit

Manzei
(Japan, 8th century)

"To what shall I liken this life?"

To what shall I liken this life?
   It is like a boat,
Which, unmoored at morn,
   Drops out of sight

And leaves no trace
    behind.

—translated from the Japanese by the Iwanami Shoten

Martial
(Hispania, 38–c. 103)

"To read my book the Virgin she"

To read my book the Virgin she
    May blush while Brutus standeth by,
But when he's gone, read through what's writ,
    And never stain a cheek for it.

—translated from the Latin by Robert Herrick

"He unto whom thou art so partial"

He unto whom thou art so partial,
    Oh, reader! is the well-known Martial,
The Epigrammatist: while living,
    Give him the fame thou wouldst be giving;
So shall he hear, and feel, and know it—
    Post-obits rarely reach a poet.

—translated from the Latin by Lord Byron, George Gordon

Mayura
(India, 7th century)

"With her left hand doing up her heavy hair"

With her left hand doing up her heavy hair,
            on which few
            flowers now remain,
And with her right holding up
            her upper garment, her girdle,
            whose cord had slipped down
During love, and her betel;
            with blooming face, with disheveled hair,
            with passion sated,
Coming forth from the private chamber,
            having yielded to the power of love,
            she longs for the breeze.

"Who is this maiden..."

Who is this maiden
    that has been enjoyed and then let go,
        and who, with wandering glance,
            and with garments clinging to her limbs with
                perspiration,
At dawn goes here and there, timid and distrustful, like
    a gazelle?
    How is this?

Has this lotus face, with its lower lip's welling nectar,
    been sipped by a bee?
By whom has heaven been enjoyed today?

With whom has Kama,
  once slain by Siva's eye,
   been pleased?

"Who is this timid gazelle"

Who is this timid gazelle,
  with a burden of firm, swelling breasts,
With roving glance, and slender of waist,
  gone forth from the frightened herd?
She goes as if she were fallen from the temple of a
  rutting lord of elephants.

Seeing this form, with its adornment of beautiful limbs,
  even an old man becomes a Kama.

Meleager
(Greece, 1st century B.C.)

Mosquitoes

Shrill-screaming mosquitoes, you shameless
  bloodthirsty bloodsuckers,
  two-winged night devils!
Leave, I beg you, quiet Zenophila,
  to her tranquil sleep.
  Eat me instead!

Oh, why bother asking?
  Even these relentless unfeeling beasts
  prefer her sweet flesh.

But listen up, evil swarm! You've been warned:
    Cease your boldness!
    Or you'll feel the force of jealous hands.

—translated from the Greek by Bob Blaisdell

"The cup rejoiceth in its pride"

The cup rejoiceth in its pride,
    And gladly does attest
    That to my girl's melodious mouth
It has been often pressed.

But would that she might lay her lips
    On mine, O happy cup!
    And drawing forth my inmost soul
At one draught drink it up.

—translated from the Greek by Jane Minot Sedgwick

"Oh, ye bitter waves of Love"

Oh, ye bitter waves of Love,
Restless blasts of jealousy,
Wintry seas of reveling,
    Whither are you bearing me?

All the rudders of my heart
Are unloosened from the helm:
Is insidious Scylla doomed
    Me again to overwhelm?

—translated from the Greek by Jane Minot Sedgwick

"I made haste to escape from Love"

I made haste to escape from Love;
  but he, lighting a little torch from the ashes,
    found me in hiding.

He bent not his bow,
  but the tips of his thumb and finger,
    and breaking off a pinch of fire
secretly threw it at me.

And from thence the flames
  rose about me on all sides.

O Phanion,
  little light that set ablaze
    in my heart
a great fire.

    —*translated from* The Greek Anthology *by W. R. Paton*

"Pain has begun to touch my heart"

Pain has begun to touch my heart,
  for hot Love, as he strayed,
    scratched it with the tip of his nails,
      and, smiling, said,

"Again, O unhappy lover,
  thou shalt have the sweet wound,
    burnt by biting honey."

Since when, seeing among the youths
   the fresh sapling Diophantus,
      I can neither fly nor abide.

—*translated from* The Greek Anthology *by W. R. Paton*

George Meredith
(England, 1828–1909)

"They have no song, the sedges dry"

They have no song, the sedges dry,
   And still they sing.
It is within my breast they sing,
   As I pass by.
Within my breast they touch a string,
   They wake a sigh.
There is but sound of sedges dry;
   In me they sing.

Czeslaw Milosz
(Lithuania/Poland/U.S.A., 1911–2004)

Gift

A day so happy.
Fog lifted early, I worked in the garden.
Hummingbirds were stopping over honeysuckle flowers.
There was no thing on earth I wanted to possess.
I knew no one worth my envying him.
Whatever evil I had suffered, I forgot.

To think that once I was the same man did not
    embarrass me.
In my body I felt no pain.
When straightening up, I saw the blue sea and sails.

Berkeley, 1971.

Otomo Miyori
(Japan, d. 774)

"You seem to have lived, my lady"

You seem to have lived, my lady,
    In the Land of Eternity.
You have grown younger
Than when so many years ago
                I saw you last.

—translated from the Japanese by the Iwanami Shoten

Thomas Moore
(Ireland, 1779–1852)

An Argument

I've oft been told by learned friars,
    That wishing and the crime are one,
And Heaven punishes desires
    As much as if the deed were done.

If wishing damns us, you and I
    Are damned to all our heart's content;

Come, then, at least we may enjoy
  Some pleasure for our punishment!

Edward Morike
(Germany, 1804–1875)

Think of It, My Soul!

A little fir tree is in green leaf,
  Who knows where, in the forest;
A rose bush, who can say
  In which garden?
They are already chosen,
  Think of it, my soul!
To take root on your grave
  And grow there.

Two black colts are grazing
  In the meadow;
They return home to the city
  In lively capers.
They will tread a slow pace
  With your corpse,
Perhaps, perhaps even before
  The iron that I see
Flashing on their hooves
  Becomes loose!

—*translated from the German by Stanley Appelbaum*

Arakida Moritake
(Japan, 1472–1549)

"A fallen blossom"

A fallen blossom
            returning to the bough, I thought—
But no, a butterfly.

—translated from the Japanese by Steven D. Carter

Nikolai Nekrasov
(Russia, 1821–1877)

The Capitals Are Rocked

The capitals are rocked with thunder
    Of orators in wordy feuds.
But in the depths of Russia, yonder
    An age-old awful silence broods.

Only the wind in wayside willows,
    Coming and going, does not cease;
And corn-stalks touch in curving billows
    The earth that cherishes and pillows,
Through endless fields of changeless peace.

*—translated from the Russian by Babette Deutsch and
Avrahm Yarmolinsky*

In My Country (The Serf Speaks)

Luxuriant corn of these my native fields,
    Forbidden fare you thrive:

You grow and radiant ears your blossom yields,
 While I am scarce alive.
How strange that I, a creature too of heaven
 (Such fate doth me befall),
See corn, that by my servile toil has thriven,
 Profit me not at all.

—translated from the Russian by Percy Ewing Matheson

Farewell

Farewell, think not of days that failed,
 Anger, despair, and tumult hot,
Of days when jealous darts assailed —
 The storm and tears remember not,
But days when love for me and you
 Arose a radiant star and kind,
Days when life's path ran smooth and true —
 Bless these and keep them still in mind.

—translated from the Russian by Percy Ewing Matheson

Ivan Savvich Nikitin
(Russia, 1824–1861)

A Night in a Village

Sultry air, the smoke of shavings,
Dirt spread over all,
Feet and benches dirty; cobwebs
To adorn the wall:
Smoke-begrimed each cottage chamber;
Bread and water stale;

Spinners coughing, children crying—
Want and woe prevail.
Hand to mouth lifelong they labor,
Then a pauper's grave—
Ah!what need to learn the lesson—
"Trust, my soul, be brave!"

—*translated from the Russian by Percy Ewing Matheson*

Princess Nukada
(Japan, 630–690)

"While waiting for you"

While waiting for you
My heart is filled with longing.
The autumn wind blows—
As if it were you—
Swaying the bamboo blinds of my
door.

—*translated from the Japanese by the Iwanami Shoten*

Abu Nuwas
(Persia/Arabia, c. 756–c. 814)

"Four things banish grief and care"

Four things banish grief and care,
Four sweet things incline
Body and soul and eyne
To enjoy, if they be there:

Water, wine,
Gardens bright and faces fair.

—translated from the Arabic by Reynold A. Nicholson

"Ho! a cup, and fill it up, and tell me it is wine"

Ho! a cup, and fill it up, and tell me it is wine,
For never will I drink in shade if I can drink in shine.
Curst and poor is every hour that sober I must go,
But rich am I when'er well drunk I stagger to and fro.
Speak, for shame, the loved one's name, let vain
    disguises fall;
Good for naught are pleasures hid behind a curtain-wall.

—translated from the Arabic by Reynold A. Nicholson

Nikolay Ogarev
(Russia, 1813–1877)

The Road

Faint shines the far moon
    Through misty night,
    Sad lies the dead field
    In the moon's light.

White with frost along
    The road without end,
    Bare-branched their long line
    Birches extend.

Bells tinkle, the team
   Swiftly whirls along,
   My drowsy driver hums
   Softly his song.

Onward I travel
   In my crazy cart,
   Sadly, pitying
   The land of my heart.

—*translated from the Russian by Percy Ewing Matheson*

Prince Otsu and Lady Ishikawa
(Japan, 663–686; unknown)

"Waiting for you"

He:

        Waiting for you,
        In the dripping dew of the hill
        I stood,—weary and wet
        With the dripping dew of the hill.

She:

        Would I had been, beloved,
        The dripping dew of the hill,
        That wetted you
        While for me you waited.

Octavio Paz
(Mexico, 1914–1998)

Touch

My hands draw
   the curtains of you
      Cover you in another nakedness
Discover the bodies of your body
   My hands
      create another body of your body.

—*translated from the Spanish by Bob Blaisdell*

George Peele
(England, c. 1558–c. 1596)

Song of Bethsabe Bathing

Hot sun, cool fire, tempered with sweet air,
   Black shade, fair nurse, shadow my white hair:
Shine, sun; burn, fire; breathe, air, and ease me;
   Black shade, fair nurse, shroud me, and please me:
Shadow, my sweet nurse, keep me from burning,
   Make not my glad cause cause of my mourning.

Let not my beauty's fire
   Inflame unstaid desire,
Nor pierce any bright eye
   That wandereth lightly.

Gyorgy Petri
(Hungary, 1943–2000)

To Be Said Over and Over Again

I glance down at my shoe and—there's the lace!
This can't be gaol then, can it, in that case.

—*translated from the Hungarian by Clive Wilmer and*
    George Gomori

"I am stuck, Lord, on your hook"

I am stuck, Lord, on your hook.
I've been wriggling there, curled up,
for the past twenty-six years,
alluringly, and yet the line has never gone taut.
It's now clear
there are no fish in your river.
If you still have hopes, Lord, choose
another worm. It's been truly
beautiful,
being among the elect.
All the same, now I'd just like to
dry off, and loaf about in the sun.

—*translated from the Hungarian by Clive Wilmer and*
    George Gomori

Caius Petronius
(Rome, c. 27–66)

"Doing, a filthy pleasure is, and short"

Doing, a filthy pleasure is, and short;
   And done, we straight repent us of the sport:
Let us not then rush blindly on unto it,
   Like lustful beasts, that only know to do it:
For lust will languish, and that heat decay.
   But thus, thus, keeping endless holiday,
Let us together closely lie and kiss,
   There is no labour, nor no shame in this;
This hath pleas'd, doth please, and long will please; never
   Can this decay, but is beginning ever.

—*translated from the Latin by Ben Jonson*

Li Po
(China, 701–762)

Taking Leave of a Friend

Blue mountains to the north of the walls,
White river winding about them;
Here we must make separation
And go out through a thousand miles of dead grass.
Mind like a floating white cloud,
Sunset like the parting of old acquaintances
Who bow over their clasped hands at a distance.
Our horses neigh to each other
   as we are departing.

—*translated from the Chinese by Ezra Pound*

Still Night Thoughts

Moonlight in front of my bed—
I took it for frost on the ground!
I lift my eyes to watch the mountain moon,
lower them and dream of home.

—translated from the Chinese by Burton Watson

A Night with a Friend

Dousing clean a thousand old cares,
sticking it out through a hundred pots of wine,
a good night needing the best of conversation,
a brilliant moon that will not let us sleep—
drunk we lie down in empty hills,
heaven and earth our quilt and pillow.

—translated from the Chinese by Burton Watson

Autumn Cove

At Autumn Cove, so many white monkeys,
bounding, leaping up like snowflakes in flight!
They coax and pull their young ones down from the
    branches
to drink and frolic with the water-borne moon.

—translated from the Chinese by Burton Watson

Ezra Pound
(U.S.A., 1885–1972)

In a Station of the Metro

The apparition of these faces in the crowd;
Petals on a wet, black bough.

Couplet

Drawing a sword, cut into water, water again flow.
Raise cup, quench sorrow, sorrow again sorry.

The Garret

Come, let us pity those who are better off than we are.
Come, my friend, and remember
        that the rich have butlers and no friends,
And we have friends and no butlers.
Come, let us pity the married and the unmarried.

Dawn enters with little feet
        like a gilded Pavlova
And I am near my desire.
Nor has life in it aught better
Than this hour of clear coolness
        the hour of waking together.

Το Καλον

Even in my dreams you have denied yourself to me
And sent me only your handmaids.

Alba

As cool as the pale wet leaves
Of lily-of-the-valley
She lay beside me in the dawn.

Chanson Arabe

I have shaken with love half the night
The winter rain falls in the street
She is but half my age;
  Whither, whither am I going?
I have shaken with love half the night.
She is but half my age.
  Whither, whither am I going?

Alexander Pushkin
(Russia, 1799–1837)

I Loved You

Loved you, I did, may even love you still;
My heart's fire's not cold:
But don't let *that* bother you;
I've no wish to sadden you at all.
Loved you, I did, wordlessly, hopelessly,
Tormented so by jealousy.
Loved you, I did, so truly, so dearly:
Let God grant you another such love.

  —translated from the Russian by Bob Blaisdell

Work

Here is the long-bided hour: the labor of years is
        accomplished.
    Why should this sadness unplumbed secretly weigh
        on my heart?
Is it, my work being done, I stand like a laborer, useless,
    One who has taken his pay, a stranger to tasks that
        are new?
Is it the work I regret, the silent companion of midnight,
    Friend of the golden-haired Dawn, friend of the gods
        of the hearth?

—translated from the Russian by Babette Deutsch and
  Avrahm Yarmolinsky

Francis Quarles
(England, 1592–1644)

On the World

The world's an inn; and I her guest.
    I eat; I drink; I take my rest.
My hostess, nature, does deny me
    Nothing, wherewith she can supply me;
Where, having stayed a while, I pay
    Her lavish bills, and go my way.

Rafi of Merv
(Persia, 12th century)

The Roses of Thy Cheeks

The roses of thy cheeks at last will fade and languish,
At last this lovelorn heart will throb no more in anguish.
Why buildest thou so much on fortune's passing favor?
    Ere long thy sun will set and disappear for ever.

Thy beauty and my love—the love thou art still
        disdaining—
In the glinting of an eye they leave no trace remaining,
Deal not in wounds nor drive a busy trade of sorrow!
    Thy mart is thronged today, but few will come
        tomorrow.

—translated from the Arabic by Reynold A. Nicholson

Anthony Raftery
(Ireland, 1784–1835)

I Am Raftery

I am Raftery the Poet
Full of hope and love,
With eyes that have no light,
With gentleness that has no misery.

Going west upon my pilgrimage
By the light of my heart,
Feeble and tired
To the end of my road.

Behold me now,
And my face to the wall,
A-playing music
Unto empty pockets.

—translated from the Irish by Douglas Hyde

Walter Raleigh
(England, 1552–1618)

Epitaph

Even such is time, which takes in trust
   Our youth, our joys, and all we have,
And pays us but with age and dust,
   Who in the dark and silent grave
When we have wandered all our ways
   Shuts up the story of our days,
And from which earth, and grave, and dust
   The Lord will raise me up, I trust.

Mathurin Régnier
(France, 1573-1613)

His Epitaph

I've lived my life sans stress or care,
Wandering freely here and there,
For I to Nature's laws defer.
And so I am astonished now,
That Death has deigned to think somehow
Of me, who never thought of her.

—translated from the French by Dorothy Belle Pollack

Abraham Reisen
(Russia, U.S.A., 1876–1953)

Healing

Kiss my grey hair, oh, my love,
You may yet
Kiss away the grey, and bring
Back the jet.

Kiss the anguish from my eye,
And the doubt;
I may yet turn good again,
And devout.

Kiss the venom, oh, my love
From my tongue,
And perhaps I'll be a fool
Again, and young.

—*translated from the Yiddish by Joseph Leftwich*

Rainer Maria Rilke
(Bohemia, 1875–1926)

The Panther
(In the Jardin des Plantes, Paris)

From walking past the bars his eyes
    have grown so tired, they retain nothing more.
It seems to him there are a thousand bars
    and, behind those thousand bars, no world.

His soft walk, with lithe and strong steps,
    turning in the smallest possible circle,
is like a dance of force around a midpoint
    in which a mighty will stands benumbed.

Only at times is the curtain of his pupils
    noiselessly raised. — Then an image enters,
passes through the tensed calm of his limbs —
    and in his heart ceases to be.

—*translated from the German by Stanley Appelbaum*

Arthur Rimbaud
(France, 1854–1891)

Departure

Enough seen. The vision was met with in every clime.
Enough had. Sounds of cities, in the evening, and in the
    sun, and always.
Enough known. The decrees of life. — O Sounds and
    Visions!
Departure in new affection and new noise!

—*translated from the French by Stanley Appelbaum*

Sensation

On the blue summer evenings, I shall walk down the
paths, pricked by the standing grain, treading the fine
grass: dreamily, I shall feel its coolness on my feet.
I shall let the wind bathe my bare head.

I won't speak, I shall have no thoughts: but infinite love will well up in my soul, and I shall go far, very far, like a Gypsy, through Nature,—as happy as if I were with a woman.

—translated from the French by Stanley Appelbaum

Theodore Roethke
(U.S.A., 1908–1963)

Heard in a Violent Ward

In heaven too,
You'd be institutionalized.
But that's all right,—
If they let you eat and swear
With the likes of Blake
And Christopher Smart,
And that sweet man John Clare.

Emile Roumer
(Haiti, 1903–1988)

The Peasant Declares His Love

High-yellow of my heart, with breasts like tangerines,
you taste better to me than eggplant stuffed with crab,
you are the tripe in my pepper-pot,
the dumpling in my peas, my tea of aromatic herbs.
You are the corned beef whose customhouse is my heart,
my mush with syrup that trickles down the throat.

You are a steaming dish, mushroom cooked with rice,
crisp potato fries, and little fish fried brown...
My hankering for love follows you wherever you go.
Your bum is a gorgeous basket brimming with fruits
    and meat.

—translated from the French by John Peale Bishop

Conrado Nale Roxlo
(Argentina, 1898–1971)

The Unforseen

Lord never grant me what I ask for.
The unforeseen delights me, what comes down
from your fair stars; let life
deal out before me all at once the cards

against which I must play. I want the shock
of going silently along my dark street,
feeling that I am tapped upon the shoulder,
turning about, and seeing the face of adventure.

I do not want to know where and how
I shall meet death. Caught unaware,
may my soul learn at the turn of a corner
that one step back it still lived.

—translated from the Spanish by Milton Ben Davis

Rufinus
(Greece, 1st–6th century)

"I am armed with the breastplate of reason"

I am armed with the breastplate of reason
    To battle with Eros alone;
And I know that he never can conquer
    In the warfare of one against one.

Though mortal matched with an immortal,
    I care not, yet what could I do
If he should bring Baccus to help him,
    And I were but one against two?

—translated from the Greek by Jane Minot Sedgwick

Edna St. Vincent Millay
(U.S.A., 1892–1950)

First Fig

My candle burns at both ends;
It will not last the night;
But, ah, my foes, and oh, my friends —
It gives a lovely light.

Eel-Grass

No matter what I say,
    All that I really love
Is the rain that flattens on the bay,
    And the eel-grass in the cove;

The jingle-shells that lie and bleach
   At the tide-line, and the trace
Of higher tides along the beach:
   Nothing in this place.

❧

Lady Otomo no Sakanoye
(Japan, 8th century)

"My heart, thinking"

My heart, thinking
"How beautiful he is"
is like a swift river
which though one dams it and dams it
will still break through.

—translated from the Japanese by Arthur Waley

❧

Carl Sandburg
(U.S.A., 1878–1967)

Fog

The fog comes
on little cat feet.

It sits looking
over harbor and city
on silent haunches
and then moves on.

❧

Sappho
(Greece, 612 B.C.?–557 B.C.)

A Young Bride

Like the sweet apple
which reddens upon the topmost bough,
    A-top on the topmost twig —
        which the pluckers forgot somehow —

Forgot it not, nay,
    but got it not,
        for none could get it till now.

—translated from the Greek by Dante Gabriel Rossetti

"My muse, what ails this ardor?"

My muse, what ails this ardor?
  Mine eyes be dim, my limbs shake,
  My voice is hoarse, my throat scorcht,
My tongue to this roof cleaves,

My fancy amazed, my thoughts dulled,
  My head doth ache, my life faints
  My soul begins to take leave,
So great a passion all feel,
  To think a soar so deadly
  I should so rashly rip up.

—translated from the Greek by Phillip Sidney

William Shakespeare
(England, 1564–1616)

"Where the bee sucks, there suck I"

Where the bee sucks, there suck I;
In a cowslip's bell I lie;
There I couch when owls do cry.
On the bat's back I do fly
After summer merrily.
Merrily, merrily shall I live now
Under the blossom that hangs on the bough.

"Under the greenwood tree"

Under the greenwood tree
Who loves to lie with me,
And turn his merry note
Unto the sweet bird's throat,
Come hither, come hither, come hither:
Here shall he see no enemy
But winter and rough weather.

"Full fathom five thy father lies"

Full fathom five thy father lies;
Of his bones are coral made;
Those are pearls that were his eyes:
Nothing of him that doth fade
But doth suffer a sea-change
Into something rich and strange.

Sea-nymphs hourly ring his knell:
Ding-dong.
Hark! now I hear them,—ding-dong, bell.

Percy Bysshe Shelley
(England, 1792–1822)

To ——

Music, when soft voices die,
Vibrates in the memory;
Odors, when sweet violets sicken,
Live within the sense they quicken.

Rose leaves, when the rose is dead,
Are heaped for the beloved's bed;
And so thy thoughts, when thou art gone,
Love itself shall slumber on.

Masoka Shiki
(Japan, 1867–1902)

"Snow's falling"

Snow's falling
I see it through a hole
In the shutter.

—*translated from the Japanese by Janine Beichman*

James Shirley
(England, 1596–1666)

Good-night

Bid me no more good-night; because
      'Tis dark, must I away?
Love doth acknowledge no such laws,
      And Love 'tis I obey,
Which, blind, doth all your light despise,
      And hath no need of eyes
            When day is fled;
      Besides, the sun, which you
      Complain is gone, 'tis true,
            Is gone to bed:
      Oh, let us do so too.

On Her Dancing

I stood and saw my mistress dance,
   Silent, and with so fixed an eye,
Some might suppose me in a trance.
   But being asked why,
By one who knew I was in love,
   I could not but impart
My wonder, to behold her move
   So nimbly with a marble heart.

Philip Sidney
(England, 1554–1586)

The Bargain

My true love hath my heart, and I have his,
By just exchange one for another given:
I hold his dear, and mine he cannot miss,
There never was a better bargain driven:
    My true love hath my heart, and I have his.

His heart in me keeps him and me in one,
My heart in him his thoughts and senses guides:
He loves my heart, for once it was his own,
I cherish his because in me it bides:
    My true love hath my heart, and I have his.

Iio Sogi
(Japan, 1421–1502)

"Everything that was"

        everything that was
    has vanished from my aged heart
        leaving not a trace

—*translated from the Japanese by Earl Miner*

Yamazaki Sokan
(Japan, 1464–1552)

"O Moon!"

> O Moon!—if we
> Should put a handle to you,
> What a fan you'd be!

—translated from the Japanese by Harold Gould Henderson

Georgios Souris
(Greece, 1852–1919)

Ode to Coffee

Oh, my heavy sweet coffee
alone
or with friends
each sip of you
comes with a lofty idea.

—translated from the Greek by Karen Van Dyck

Gertrude Stein
(U.S.A., 1874–1946)

I Am Rose

I am Rose; my eyes are blue
I am Rose and who are you
I am Rose and when I sing
I am Rose like anything.

Alan Stephens
(U.S.A., 1925–2009)

Watching the Shorebirds That Winter Here

> "…*the limits and the lack*
> *Set in their finished features.*"
> —W.H. Auden

They are exactly
as intelligent as

they need to be, to
be what they are: having

limits, but no lack,
in their physical

perfection, each is, in
each detail, on close

inspection a wonder and
matter-of-fact. *Clear-*

ly clearly clearly cry
some curlews flying by

us assorted humans here.

A Last Time

He still has poems to write
but that region of his mind
which got busy and mobilized
the words, will not budge now.

It's like an old saddle horse
that has stopped on his own.
The rider puts a heel
to the flank. The horse stands there,

then turns his head back around,
rolling an eye at his rider
as if to say, You ought to know
that if I could I'd go on.

Wallace Stevens
(U.S.A., 1879–1955)

The Worms at Heaven's Gate

Out of the tomb, we bring Badroulbadour,
Within our bellies, we her chariot.
Here is an eye. And here are, one by one,
The lashes of that eye and its white lid.
Here is the cheek on which that lid declined,
And, finger after finger, here, the hand,
The genius of that cheek. Here are the lips,
The bundle of the body and the feet.

.   .   .   .

Out of the tomb we bring Badroulbadour.

Anecdote of the Jar

I placed a jar in Tennessee,
And round it was, upon a hill.
It made the slovenly wilderness
Surround that hill.

The wilderness rose up to it,
And sprawled around, no longer wild.
The jar was round upon the ground
And tall and of a port in air.

It took dominion everywhere.
The jar was gray and bare.
It did not give of bird or bush,
Like nothing else in Tennessee.

Disillusionment of Ten O'Clock

The houses are haunted
By white night-gowns.
None are green,
Or purple with green rings,
Or green with yellow rings,
Or yellow with blue rings.
None of them are strange,
With socks of lace
And beaded ceintures.
People are not going
To dream of baboons and periwinkles.
Only, here and there, an old sailor,
Drunk and asleep in his boots,
Catches Tigers
In red weather.

The Wind Shifts

This is how the wind shifts:
Like the thoughts of an old human,
Who still think eagerly
And despairingly.

The wind shifts like this:
Like a human without illusions,
Who still feels irrational things within her.
The wind shifts like this:
Like humans approaching proudly,
Like humans approaching angrily.
This is how the wind shifts:
Like a human, heavy and heavy,
Who does not care.

Strato
(Greece, 2nd century)

"How shall I know..."

How shall I know when the prime
   Of my fair one is finished and over,
If I live by her side all the time,
   And am loyal and true as a lover?

Shall yesterday's joy that was mine
   This morning be turned into sorrow?
And, today, if I think her divine,
   Why should not I think so tomorrow?

—*translated from* The Greek Anthology *by Jane Minot
   Sedgwick*

"Seek not to hide our love"

Seek not to hide our love,
   Philocrates;
     the god himself without that
     hath sufficient power to trample on my heart.

But give me a taste of a blithe kiss.
   The time shall come
     when thou
     shalt beg such favor from others.

   —translated from The Greek Anthology *by W. R. Paton*

"How long shall we steal kisses"

How long shall we steal kisses
   and covertly signal to each other
with chary eyes?

How long shall we talk without coming
   to a conclusion,
linking again and again
   idle deferment to deferment?

If we tarry we shall waste the good;
   but before the envious ones come,
Phidon, let us add deeds to words.

   —translated from The Greek Anthology *by W. R. Paton*

"Happy little book"

Happy little book,
   I grudge it thee not;
     some boy reading thee will rub thee,
holding thee under his chin,
   or press thee against his delicate lips,
   or will roll thee up resting on his tender thighs,
       O most blessed of books.

Often shalt thou betake thee into his bosom,
  or, tossed down on his chair,
    shalt dare to touch without fear,
and thou shalt talk much before him all alone with him;
  but I supplicate thee, little book,
    speak something not unoften on my behalf.

—*translated from* The Greek Anthology *by W. R. Paton*

"Perchance someone in future years"

Perchance someone in future years,
    listening to these trifles of mine,
        will think these pains of love
were all my own.

No! I ever scribble this
    and that for this and
        that boy-lover,
    since some god
            gave me this gift.

—*translated from* The Greek Anthology *by W. R. Paton*

John Suckling
(England, 1609–1642)

Song

Why so pale and wan, fond lover?
  Prithee, why so pale? —
Will, when looking well can't move her,
Looking ail prevail?
  Prithee, why so pale?

Why so dull and mute, young sinner?
    Prithee, why so mute? —
Will, when speaking well can't win her,
Saying nothing do't?
    Prithee, why so mute?

Quit, quit, for shame! this will not move,
    This cannot take her —
If of herself she will not love,
Nothing can make her:
    The Devil take her!

&

Jonathan Swift
(Ireland, 1667–1745)

Verses Made for Women Who Cry Apples, etc.

Apples

Come buy my fine wares
Plums, apples and pears,
A hundred a penny,
In conscience too many:
Come, will you have any?
My children are seven,
I wish them in Heaven;
My husband's a sot,
With his pipe and his pot,
Nor a farthing will gain 'em,
And I must maintain 'em.

Herrings

Be not sparing
Leave off swearing:
Buy my herring
Fresh from Malahide,
Better ne'er was tried.
Come eat 'em with pure fresh butter and mustard,
Their bellies are soft, and as white as a custard.
Come, sixpence a dozen to get me some bread,
Or, like my own herrings, I soon shall be dead.

Otomo Tabito
(Japan, 665–731)

In Praise of Sake

Far better, it seems, than uttering pompous words
     And looking wise,
To drink sake and weep drunken tears.

❉

If I could but be happy in this life,
   What should I care if in the next
      I became a bird or a worm!

—*translated from the Japanese by the Iwanami Shoten*

Torquato Tasso
(Italy, 1544–1595)

"I would like to be a bee"

I would like to be a bee,
    Beautiful and cruel woman,
Which, buzzing, would suck the honey out of you,
And, unable to sting your heart, might at least
    Sting your white bosom
        And in so sweet a hurt
Depart its own life, avenged.

—*translated from the Italian by Bob Blaisdell*

Sara Teasdale
(U.S.A., 1884–1933)

The Kiss

I hoped that he would love me,
    And he has kissed my mouth,
But I am like a stricken bird
    That cannot reach the south.

For though I know he loves me,
    Tonight my heart is sad;
His kiss was not so wonderful
    As all the dreams I had.

Alfred, Lord Tennyson
(England, 1809–1892)

"Come not, when I am dead"

Come not, when I am dead,
    To drop thy foolish tears upon my grave,
To trample round my fallen head,
    And vex the unhappy dust thou wouldst not save.
There let the wind sweep and the plover cry;
        But thou, go by.

Child, if it were thine error or thy crime
    I care no longer, being all unblest:
Wed whom thou wilt, but I am sick of Time,
    And I desire to rest.
Pass on, weak heart, and leave me where I lie:
        Go by, go by.

Henry David Thoreau
(U.S.A., 1817–1862)

My Life Has Been the Poem

My life has been the poem I would have writ
But I could not both live and utter it.

John Todhunter
(Ireland, 1839–1916)

Song

Bring from the craggy haunts of birch and pine,
    Thou wild wind, bring
Keen forest odors from that realm of thine,
        Upon thy wing!

Oh! wind, Oh! mighty, melancholy wind,
    Blow through me, blow!
Thou blowest forgotten things into my mind,
        From long ago.

Marina Tsvetaeva
(Russia, 1892–1941)

"I do not think, or argue, or complain"

I do not think, or argue, or complain.
Or sleep.
I long for neither sun, nor moon, nor sea.
Nor ship.

I do not feel the heat amidst these walls,
Nor garden's green,
Nor do I long for your desired gift,
Foreseen.

Neither the morning gladdens nor the trolley's
Ring-singing run.
I live, forgetting date and age
And daylight sun.

I am—a dancer on a tightrope slashed
And hewn.
I am—a shadow's shadow: lunatic
Of two dark moons.

—translated from the Russian by Ekaterina Rogalskaya

"They fly–quick-wrought and quickly written"

They fly—quick-wrought and quickly written,
Still hot from all the bitterness and bliss.
My moment, hour, day, year, lifetime—smitten,
Twixt love and love lie on the crucifix.

And I hear word of thunderstorms a-rising;
Spears, Amazonian, again flash through the sky...
Yet cannot hold my pen back! These two roses
Have sucked my heart's blood dry.

—translated from the Russian by Ekaterina Rogalskaya

"The gypsy passion of parting!"

The gypsy passion of parting!
Brief encounter and—you fly hence!
Head into hands dropping,
I think, with a night-ward glance

That no one, unearthing our letters,
Had understood the depth
Of our treachery, that is—
How true we had been to ourselves.

—translated from the Russian by Ekaterina Rogalskaya

Su Tung-p'o
(China, 1036–1101)

Spring Night

Spring night—one hour worth a thousand gold coins;
clear scent of flowers, shadowy moon.
Songs and flutes upstairs—threads of sound;
in the garden, a swing, where night is deep and still.

—translated from the Chinese by Burton Watson

On the Birth of His Son

Families, when a child is born,
Want it to be intelligent.
I, through intelligence,
Having wrecked my whole life,
Only hope the baby will prove
Ignorant and stupid.
Then he will crown a tranquil life
By becoming a Cabinet Minister.

—translated from the Chinese by Arthur Waley

Fyodor Tyutchev
(Russia, 1803–1873)

Holy Russia

A Beggar's hut, a countryside
    Not blest with wealth or grand,
A country by long suffering tried,
    Russia, my native land!

The foreigner with scornful gaze
   Nor sees nor heeds the wealth
That glimmers through your hidden ways
   And humbly flowers by stealth.

The Lord of heaven His cross who bore,
   My land beyond compare,
A Servant walked your acres o'er
   And left His blessing there.

—translated from the Russian by Percy Ewing Matheson

Paul Verlaine
(France, 1844–1896)

Autumn Song

The wailings of Autumn's
    Violins
Pierce through my heart,
    Where dull languor begins.

All pale and wan,
    As when tolls the bell,
I think of the past,
    And I weep for its knell.

And I go, as the wind
    Carries me ahead,
Straying here, straying there,
    Like a leaf that is dead.

—translated from the French by Dorothy Belle Pollack

Gil Vicente
(Portugal, c. 1465–c. 1536)

Song

If thou art sleeping, maiden,
    Awake and open thy door.
'Tis the break of day, and we must away
    O'er meadow, and mount, and moor.

Wait not to find thy slippers,
    But come with thy naked feet;
We shall have to pass through the dewy grass
    And waters wide and fleet.

—*translated from the Portuguese by Henry Wadsworth*
    Longfellow

Edmund Waller
(England, 1606–1687)

On a Girdle

That which her slender waist confin'd,
    Shall now my joyful temples bind;
    No monarch but would give his crown,
His arms might do what this has done.

It was my heaven's extremest sphere,
    The pale which held that lovely deer,
    My joy, my grief, my hope, my love,
Did all within this circle move.

A narrow compass, and yet there
   Dwelt all that's good, and all that's fair;
   Give me but what this ribbon bound,
Take all the rest the sun goes round.

Wang Wei
(China, 699?–761)

Deer Fence

Empty hills, no one in sight,
only the sound of someone talking;
late sunlight enters the deep wood,
shining over the green moss again.

—translated from the Chinese by Burton Watson

Duckweed Pond

By the spring pond, deep and wide,
you must be waiting for the light boat to return.
Supple and soft, the green duckweed meshes,
till dangling willows sweep it open again.

—translated from the Chinese by Burton Watson

Walt Whitman
(U.S.A., 1819–1892)

The Last Invocation

At the last, tenderly,
From the walls of the powerful fortress'd house,
From the clasp of the knitted locks, from the keep of the
  well-closed doors,
Let me be wafted.

Let me glide noiselessly forth;
With the key of softness unlock the locks—with a whisper,
Set ope the doors O soul.

Tenderly—be not impatient,
(Strong is your hold O mortal flesh,
Strong is your hold O love.)

Oscar Wilde
(Ireland, 1854–1900)

Requiescat

Tread lightly, she is near
Under the snow,
Speak gently, she can hear
The daisies grow.

All her bright golden hair
Tarnished with rust,
She that was young and fair
Fallen to dust.

Lily-like, white as snow,
She hardly knew
She was a woman, so
Sweetly she grew.

Coffin-board, heavy stone,
Lie on her breast,
I vex my heart alone,
She is at rest.

Peace, peace, she cannot hear
Lyre or sonnet,
All my life's buried here,
Heap earth upon it.

William Carlos Williams
(U.S.A., 1883–1963)

The Red Wheelbarrow

so much depends
upon

a red wheel
barrow

glazed with rain
water

beside the white
chickens.

The Young Housewife

At ten AM the young housewife
moves about in negligee behind
the wooden walls of her husband's house.
I pass solitary in my car.

Then again she comes to the curb
to call the ice-man, fish-man, and stands
shy, uncorseted, tucking in
stray ends of hair, and I compare her
to a fallen leaf.

The noiseless wheels of my car
rush with a crackling sound over
dried leaves as I bow and pass smiling.

Pastoral

The little sparrows
hop ingenuously
about the pavement
quarreling
with sharp voices
over those things
that interest them.
But we who are wiser
shut ourselves in
on either hand
and no one knows
whether we think good
or evil.
Meanwhile,

the old man who goes about
gathering dog-lime
walks in the gutter
without looking up
and his tread
is more majestic than
that of the Episcopal minister
approaching the pulpit
of a Sunday.
These things
astonish me beyond words.

Willow Poem

It is a willow when summer is over,
a willow by the river
from which no leaf has fallen nor
bitten by the sun
turned orange or crimson.
The leaves cling and grow paler,
swing and grow paler
over the swirling waters of the river
as if loth to let go,
they are so cool, so drunk with
the swirl of the wind and of the river—
oblivious to winter,
the last to let go and fall
into the water and on the ground.

To Waken an Old Lady

Old age is
a flight of small

cheeping birds
skimming
bare trees
above a snow glaze.
Gaining and failing
they are buffeted
by a dark wind—
But what?
On harsh weedstalks
the flock has rested—
the snow
is covered with broken
seed husks
and the wind tempered
with a shrill
piping of plenty.

The Thinker

My wife's new pink slippers
have gay pompons.
There is not a spot or a stain
on their satin toes or their sides.
All night they lie together
under her bed's edge.
Shivering I catch sight of them
and smile, in the morning.
Later I watch them
descending the stair,
hurrying through the doors
and round the table,
moving stiffly

with a shake of their gay pompons!
And I talk to them
in my secret mind
out of pure happiness.

The Lonely Street

School is over. It is too hot
to walk at ease. At ease
in light frocks they walk the streets
to while the time away.
They have grown tall. They hold
pink flames in their right hands.
In white from head to foot,
with sidelong, idle look—
in yellow, floating stuff,
black sash and stockings—
touching their avid mouths
with pink sugar on a stick—
like a carnation each holds in her hand—
they mount the lonely street.

The Great Figure

Among the rain
and lights
I saw the figure 5
in gold
on a red
firetruck
moving
tense

unheeded
to gong clangs
siren howls
and wheels rumbling
through the dark city.

John Wilson
(U.S.A., b. 1947)

Papa's Alba

My love,
whose kisses come
crisp and hot
as bacon
off the griddle

till the sun
gets in our curtains
and the clock
saws us in two,
my love,

goodbye.
"Goodbye."

Three Haiku

Old man and his wife
same height, same weight, same hats
barefoot on the beach

❀

Fog drifts in,
wind dies down, branches moving
on their own

❋

Black against the dusk
a hawk takes its time circling
the dry river bed

☙

William Wordsworth
(England, 1770–1850)

"A slumber did my spirit seal"

A slumber did my spirit seal;
   I had no human fears;
She seemed a thing that could not feel
The touch of earthly years.

No motion has she now, no force;
   She neither hears nor sees;
Rolled round in earth's diurnal course,
With rocks, and stones, and trees.

My Heart Leaps Up

My heart leaps up when I behold
   A rainbow in the sky:
So was it when my life began;
So is it now I am a man;
So be it when I shall grow old,
   Or let me die!

The Child is father of the Man;
And I could wish my days to be
Bound each to each by natural piety.

Emperor Wu-ti
(China, 157 B.C.–87 B.C.)

Liu Ch'e

The rustling of the silk is discontinued,
Dust drifts over the court-yard,
There is no sound of foot-fall, and the leaves
Scurry into heaps and lie still,
And she the rejoicer of the heart is beneath them:

A wet leaf that clings to the threshold.

—translated from the Chinese by Ezra Pound

The Autumn Wind

Autumn wind rises; white clouds fly.
   Grass and trees wither; geese go south.
   Orchids, all in bloom; chrysanthemums smell sweet.
I think of my lovely lady; I never can forget.
   Floating-pagoda boat crosses Fen River;
   Across the midstream white waves rise.
Flute and drum keep time to sound of rowers' song;
   Amidst revel and feasting sad thoughts come;
   Youth's years how few, age how sure!

—translated from the Chinese by Arthur Waley

Li Fu-Jen

The sound of her silk skirt has stopped.
On the marble pavement dust grows.
Her empty room is cold and still.
Fallen leaves are piled against the doors.
    Longing for that lovely lady
How can I bring my aching heart to rest?

—translated from the Chinese by Arthur Waley

Otomo Yakamochi
(Japan, 716–785)

"What pain and distress"

What pain and distress
    A dream tryst brings!
  I start and wake,
    And grope in vain for you,
Beyond the reach of my hand.

—translated from the Japanese by the Iwanami Shoten

Mei Yao-ch'en
(China, 1002–1060)

At Night, Hearing Someone Sing in the House Next Door

Midnight: I still haven't gotten to sleep
when I hear faint sounds of singing next door.

I picture to myself the red lips moving;
the dust stirs on the rafters, I know.

She makes a mistake and laughs to herself.
I get up to listen and put on my robe;
put on my robe, but the song has ended.
The moon in the window shines a little while longer.

—translated from the Chinese by Burton Watson

William Butler Yeats
(Ireland, 1865–1939)

He Wishes for the Cloths of Heaven

Had I the heavens' embroidered cloths,
Enwrought with the golden and silver light,
The blue and the dim and the dark cloths
Of night and light and half-light,
I would spread the cloths under your feet
But I, being poor, have only my dreams;
I have spread my dreams beneath your feet;
Tread softly because you tread on my dreams...

A Drinking Song

Wine comes in at the mouth
And love comes in at the eye;
That's all we shall know for truth
Before we grow old and die.
I lift the glass to my mouth,
I look at you, and I sigh.

Down by the Salley Gardens

Down by the salley gardens my love and I did meet;
She pass'd the salley gardens with little snow-white feet.
She bid me take love easy, as the leaves grow on the tree;
But I, being young and foolish, with her would not agree.

In a field by the river my love and I did stand,
And on my leaning shoulder she laid her snow-white
    hand.
She bid me take life easy, as the grass grows on the
    weirs;
But I was young and foolish, and now am full of tears.

Shen Yo
(China, 441–513)

Dreaming of Her

"I heard at night your sighs
And knew that you were thinking of me."
        As she spoke, the doors of Heaven opened;
        Our souls conversed and I saw her face.

She set me a pillow to rest on;
She brought me meat and drink.
        I stood beside her where she lay,
        But suddenly woke and she was not there.

And none knew how my soul was torn,
    How the tears fell surging over my breast.

—translated from the Chinese by Arthur Waley

Bibliography

Abu'l-Ala al-Ma'rri. *The Quatrains of Abu'l-Ala*. New York: Doubleday & Co., 1903.

Mary Barnard. *Collected Poems*. Portland, Oregon: Breitenbush Books, 1979.

Gustavo Adolfo Becquer. *Rhymes and Legends (Selection): A Dual-Language Book.* Edited by Stanley Appelbaum. Mineola, New York: Dover, 2006.

William Blake. *Songs of Innocence and Songs of Experience*. Mineola, New York: Dover, 1997.

The Bridal Bouquet: Culled from the Garden of Literature. Henry Southgate, editor. London: Lockwood & Co., 1873.

Edward G. Browne. *A Literary History of Persia: From Firdawsi to Sa'di.* New York: Charles Scribner's Sons, 1906.

Lord Byron, George Gordon. *The Complete Poetical Works of Lord Byron.* Paul Elmer More, editor. Boston: Houghton, Mifflin, 1905.

A Century of Indian Epigrams: Chiefly from the Sanskrit of Bhartrihari. Translated by Paul Elmer More. Boston: Houghton, Mifflin and Co., 1899.

John Clare. *The Poems of John Clare*. London: J. M. Dent, 1935.

The Classic Tradition of Haiku: An Anthology. Faubion Bowers, editor. Mineola, New York: Dover, 1996.

Samuel Taylor Coleridge. *The Golden Book of Coleridge.* London: Dent, 1909.

Coloured Stars: Versions of Fifty Asiatic Love Poems. Edward Powys Mathers, editor. Boston: Houghton Mifflin Co., 1918.

The Columbia Book of Chinese Poetry: From Early Times to the Thirteenth Century. Burton Watson, editor. New York: Columbia University Press, 1984.

Corn from Olde Fieldes: An Anthology of English Poems from the XIVth to the XVIIth Century. Eleanor M. Brougham, editor. London: John Lane, 1918.

Robert Creeley. *Selected Poems*. Berkeley: University of California Press, 1991.

The Critic. New York: American News Company. March 28, 1891.

Frances Densmore. *Teton Sioux Music*. Washington, D.C.: Smithsonian Institution, Bureau of American Ethnology, 1918.

Frances Densmore. Washington, D.C.: Smithsonian Institution, Bureau of American Ethnology, *Chippewa Music,* 1913.

Emily Dickinson. *Favorite Poems*. Mineola, New York: Dover, 1990.

Paul Laurence Dunbar. *Selected Poems*. Mineola, New York: Dover, 1997.

Elizabethan Poetry. Bob Blaisdell, editor. Mineola, New York: Dover, 2005.

The Epigrammatists: A Selection from Epigrammatic Literature of Ancient, Medieval, and Modern Times. Henry Philip Dodd, editor. London: George Bell and Sons, 1875.

Epigrams: Original and Selected. Benjamin Standring, editor. London: Simpkin, Marshall, and Co., 1877.

John Gould Fletcher. *Japanese Prints*. Boston: The Four Seas Company, 1918.

Robert Frost. *The Road Not Taken and Other Poems*. Mineola, New York: Dover, 1993.

First German Reader: A Beginner's Dual-Language Book. Harry Steinhauer, editor. Mineola, New York: Dover, 2007.

Muhammad Abdul Ghani. *A History of the Persian Language and Literature at the Mughal Court*. Gregg International Publishers, 1972 (orig. 1929).

Johann Wolfgang von Goethe. *103 Great Poems: 103 Meistergedichte by Johann Wolfgang von Goethe*. Edited and translated by Stanley Appelbaum. Mineola, New York: Dover, 1999.

Great German Poems of the Romantic Era: A Dual-Language Book. Stanley Appelbaum, editor. Mineola, New York: Dover, 1995.

Great Love Poems. Shane Weller, editor. Mineola, New York: Dover, 1992.

Great Short Poems. Paul Negri, editor. Mineola, New York: Dover, 2000.

Great Short Poems from Antiquity to the Twentieth Century. Dorothy Belle Pollack, editor. Mineola, New York: Dover, 2011.

The Greek Anthology. W. R. Paton, editor. The Loeb Classical Library. London: William Heinemann, 1916.

The Greek Poets: Homer to the Present. Edited by Peter Constantine, Rachel Hadas, Edmund Keeley, and Karen Van Dyck. New York: W.W. Norton & Co., 2010.

Greek Poets in English Verse. William Hyde Appleton, editor. Boston: Houghton, Mifflin, 1894.

Francis B. Gummere. *The Popular Ballad*. Boston: Houghton, Mifflin, and Co., 1907.

Jehudah Halevi. *Jehudah Halevi: Selected Poems*. Nina Salaman, editor. Philadelphia: The Jewish Publication Society of America, 1928.

Thomas Hardy. *Hardy's Selected Poems*. Mineola, New York: Dover, 1995.

Heinrich Heine. *Poems of Heinrich Heine: Three Hundred and Twenty-five Poems*. Translated by Louis Untermeyer. New York: Henry Holt, 1917.

George Herbert. *The Works of George Herbert in Prose and Verse*. New York: John Wurtele Lovell, 1981.

Robert Herrick. *The Hesperides and Noble Numbers*. Vols. 1 & 2. New York: Charles Scribner's Sons, 1891.

Nazim Hikmet. *Poems of Nazim Hikmet*. Randy Blasing and Mutlu Konuk Blasing, editors. New York: Persea, 2002.

Holy Russia and Other Poems: Translated from the Russian. Percy Ewing Matheson, editor. Oxford: Oxford University Press, 1918.

Imagist Poetry: An Anthology. Bob Blaisdell, editor. Mineola, New York: Dover, 2011.

Introduction to French Poetry: A Dual-Language Book. Edited and translated by Stanley Appelbaum. Mineola, New York: Dover, 1969.

Introduction to German Poetry: A Dual-Language Book. Edited by Gustave Mathieu and Guy Stern. Mineola, New York: Dover, 1987.

Introduction to Spanish Poetry: A Dual-Language Book. Edited by Eugenio Florit. Mineola, New York: Dover, 1965.

Irish Verse: An Anthology. Bob Blaisdell, editor. Mineola, New York: Dover, 2001.

Ben Jonson. *Plays and Poems.* London: George Routledge, 1886.

Ben Jonson. *The Works of Ben Jonson.* William Gifford, editor, 1879.

Kabir. *Songs of Kabir.* Rabindranath Tagore, editor. Mineola, New York: Dover, 2004.

Francis La Flesche. "The Osage Tribe: The Rite of Vigil." Thirty-ninth Annual Report of the Bureau of American Ethnology, 1917–1918, Vol. 39 (1925).

D. H. Lawrence. *Amores.* New York: D. W. Huebsch, 1916.

D. H. Lawrence. *Look! We Have Come Through!* London: Chatto and Windus, 1917.

A Little Treasury of World Poetry: Translations from the Great Poets of Other Languages: 2600 B.C. to 1950 A.D. Edited by Hubert Creekmore. New York: Charles Scribner's Sons, 1952.

Federico Garcia Lorca. *Book of Poems (Selection): A Dual-Language Book.* Stanley Appelbaum, editor. Mineola, New York: Dover, 2004.

Arthur A. Macdonell. *A History of Sanskrit Literature.* New York: Appleton, 1914.

Taylor Mali. *What Learning Leaves.* Newtown, Connecticut: Hanover Press, Ltd., 2002.

Meleager. *Fifty Poems of Meleager.* Walter Headlam, editor. New York: Macmillan. 1890.

Czeslaw Milosz. *New and Collected Poems: 1931-2001.* New York: Ecco, 2001.

Native American Songs and Poems: An Anthology. Brian Swann, editor. Mineola, New York: Dover, 1996.

Nine Centuries of Spanish Literature: Nueve Siglos de Literatura Espanola: A Dual-Language Anthology. Edited by Seymour Resnick and Jeanne Pasmantier. Mineola, New York: Dover, 1994.

One Hundred and One Great American Poems. Edited by The American Poetry & Literacy Project. Mineola, New York: Dover, 1998.

One Thousand Poems from the Manyoshu: The Complete Nippon Gakujutsu Shinkokai Translation. Japanese Classics Translation Committee. Mineola, New York: Dover, 2005.

Gyorgy Petri. *Night Song of the Personal Shadow*. Northumberland, England: Bloodaxe Books, Ltd., 1991. Poems used by the permission of the translators.

Poems of Faith. Bob Blaisdell, editor. Mineola, New York: Dover, 2003.

Poems of Solace and Remembrance. Paul Negri, editor. Mineola, New York: Dover, 2001.

Rainer Maria Rilke. *Selected Poems/Ausgewählte Gedichte: A Dual-Language Book*. Edited and translated by Stanley Appelbaum. Mineola, New York: Dover, 2011.

Arthur Rimbaud. *A Season in Hell and Other Works: A Dual-Language Book*. Edited and translated by Stanley Appelbaum. Mineola, New York: Dover, 2003.

Ekaterina Rogalskaya. Poems by Akhmatova and Tsvetaeva used by permission of the translator.

A Romance in Song: Heine's Lyrical Interlude. Franklin Johnson. Boston: D. Lothrop & Co., 1884.

Edna St. Vincent Millay. *Early Poems*. Mineola, New York: Dover, 2008.

Jane Minot Sedgwick. *Sicilian Idyls and Other Verses*. Boston: Copeland and Day, 1898.

Songs for the Open Road: Poems of Travel & Adventure. Edited by The American Poetry & Literacy Project. Mineola, New York: Dover, 1999.

Songs of the Vine with a Medley for Maltworms. William G. Hutchinson, editor. London: A. H. Bullen, 1904.

Alan Stephens. *Away from the Road*. Albuquerque: Living Batch Press, 1998. Poems used by permission of the author's family.

Wallace Stevens. *The Emperor of Ice-Cream and Other Poems*. Mineola, New York: Dover, 2005.

Jonathan Swift. *The Works of Jonathan Swift*. Vol. 1. London: Henry G. Bohn, 1850.

James Thomson. *The City of Dreadful Night*. Vol. 1. London: Reeves & Turner, 1895.

Translations of Eastern Poetry and Prose. R. A. Nicholson, editor. Cambridge: Cambridge University Press, 1922.

A Treasury of Russian Verse. Avrahm Yarmolinsky, editor. New York: Macmillan, 1949.

Twelve Centuries of English Poetry and Prose. Alphonso Gerald Newcomer, editor. Chicago: Scott, Foresman and Co., 1910.

Henry Van Dyke. *The Poems of Henry Van Dyke*. New York: Charles Scribner's Sons, 1906.

The Viking Portable Library: Poets of the English Language. W. H. Auden and Norman Holmes Pearson, editors, 1953.

Arthur Waley. *A Hundred and Seventy Chinese Poems*. New York: Knopf, 1919.

Arthur Waley. *Chinese Poems*. Mineola, New York: Dover, 2000.

Arthur Waley. *Japanese Poetry: The Uta*. Oxford: Oxford University Press, 1919.

William Carlos Williams. *Al Que Quiere!* Boston: The Four Seas Co., 1917.

William Carlos Williams. *Early Poems*. Mineola, New York: Dover, 1997.

William Carlos Williams. *Sour Grapes*. Boston: The Four Seas Co., 1921.

John Wilson. Poems and translation used by permission of the author and translator.

William Wordsworth. *Favorite Poems*. Mineola, New York: Dover, 1992.

Alphabetical List of Titles and First Lines

Titles are given, in italics, only when distinct from the first lines.